Praise fo

In these days in which compromise is epidemic among professing Christians, Greg Gordon has been used of God to issue this clarion call to Christians to stand firmly and zealously for the Lord. He does so by plucking out of obscurity four stalwarts of the faith who were mightily used of God.

—ROGER ELLSWORTH, author, and pastor of
Emmaus Road Baptist Church

Greg Gordon is a spiritual sleuth who looks for the motivating factors that compelled great men and women of God to live extraordinary and meaningful lives. As he took up his pen to write the sketches you will find in this book, these are the things he is focused upon.

—STEVE GALLAGHER, Founder of Pure Life Ministries

Greg Gordon loves men who love God. This is evident in his work as founder of SermonIndex.net, and it is also evident when anyone has an opportunity to meet and talk with Greg. His appreciation of God's works in the past, of historic revivals, and of the great men and women of church history drives much of the work and ministry that Greg does. Such appreciation is evident in this book, *Uncompromising Faith,* in which Greg reminds us of the lives of George Whitefield, John Cennick, George Fox, and Henry Alline. The sketches of their lives and the lessons we can learn from them are certainly applicable to the Christian life and Christian ministry today. Our generation needs such men, now more than ever. This book can be a tonic to your soul and a blessing to your heart.

—MACK TOMLINSON, author of
In Light Of Eternity, The Life Of Leonard Ravenhill

We don't need more pop-psychology or man's opinions. We need the truth. *Uncompromising Faith* gives brief biographical sketches of great men of God from the past, and provides modern-day life-application for those of us living in the 21st century.

—ISRAEL WAYNE, founder of Family Renewal

Having researched in depth the life of George Whitefield, I am thankful for this work by my good friend, Greg Gordon. May you be enriched and transformed as you read, review, receive and respond to the work of the same divine Spirit who so powerfully worked through these men of God of yesteryear. O God, do it again!

—DAVID FORD, President,
Globe For Christ International

There is a very troubling trend in the evangelical church as a whole. Foundational doctrines such as the cross, sin, judgment, and repentance were declared openly in the early hours of church history as well as in American history—when revivals and awakenings spread across our landscape. Where are the Tyndale's and Huss' who were burned at the stake for simply declaring the truth? Where are the Luthers who, when asked to recant or face possible execution, said, "Here I stand; I can do no other"? Here are four men that answered the call...will you?

—SHANE IDLEMAN, Lead Pastor,
Westside Christian Fellowship, Lancaster, California

Greg Gordon has written a powerful book which highlights the lives of four heroic men of God and their amazing faith. Books like these work to fan the flames of our own devotional lives and stir us to a greater surrender and a fuller abandonment to the Lord of Whitefield, Fox, Cennick, and Alline. In an age where faith is routinely compromised, *Uncompromising Faith* is a clear reminder of the higher ground to which God calls all his children.

—PAUL WEST, SermonIndex.net moderator and author of
Understanding Mortification

The men whom God has used in former times are worthy of study. Greg Gordon's new book, *Uncompromising Faith*, is worthy to be studied, for in it are "pen sketches" of some of God's choice servants. Read it and be blessed!

—DR. E. A. JOHNSTON,
Author of *George Whitefield: A Definitive Biography*

UNCOMPROMISING
Faith

*Brief Pen Sketches
of George Whitefield,
John Cennick, George Fox
and Henry Alline*

GREG GORDON

KingsleyPress

Shoals, Indiana

Uncompromising Faith

Published by Kingsley Press
PO Box 973
Shoals, IN 47581
USA

Tel. (800) 971-7985
www.kingsleypress.com
E-mail: sales@kingsleypress.com

ISBN: 978-1-937428-48-8 (paperback)
ISBN: 978-1-937428-49-5 (ebook)

We make every effort to attribute the source of a quote to the correct author. If there is no acknowledgment, the author either wrote the quote or we could not determine the source. Not all quotes are referenced in the footnotes, especially if the source is identified when the quote is used.

Scripture quotations are from *The Holy Bible, New International Version®*, NIV® Copyright © 1973, 1978, 1984, 2011 by Biblica, Inc.® Used by permission. All rights reserved worldwide.

Dedication

I want to acknowledge my parents. Also I want to acknowledge mentors throughout my seventeen years of following the Lord Jesus Christ on this earth, who gave of themselves unselfishly to encourage me in service for our God: Rob Kennedy, Josh Olson, Gareth Evans, Don Courville, Charles Audette, and many others. So many have prayed, serving and helping me along the way—far too many to acknowledge here individually. Also to all the users of SermonIndex.net who have prayed and been co-laborers for the recovering of the gospel in our generation.

I want to chiefly dedicate this work to my precious wife, Brandy Gordon, who has been an example to me in living flesh of an *Uncompromising Faith*. Her encouragements and faith are reasons why this book is now in print for the glory of God.

If we displease God, does it matter whom we please? If we please him, does it matter whom we displease?

—Leonard Ravenhill

Jesus will never qualify or compromise anything he has said.

—A. W. Tozer

Contents

Preface

I remember the day as a young believer that I set out on my bike with a backpack and $100 in my pocket. Biking across the city of Toronto, full of enthusiasm and zeal to find some godly old volumes, I went to an old rare book room. Perusing the aisles, the smell of older vintage volumes permeated the air. My eyes ran across two sets that I thought were a fair value. The names were recognizable, yet my knowledge of each writer was minimal to say the least. The two sets of books were: *The Complete Works of George Fox* (eight large volumes) and *The Journals of John Wesley* (another two large volumes). Biking back to my home with a very heavy load, it was as if I had found gold itself. Over the next several months, I devoured these writings. That was the beginning of a journey that has continued to the present: to unravel and discover wonderful past commitments to Jesus Christ from preachers of old.

As I read these volumes, the gap between these shining examples of what I considered "book of Acts of Christianity" and modern-day believers widened significantly. My heart set immediately to follow these older men who seemed to really know the Lord and have *uncompromising faith!*

Trying to emulate a godly preacher from the past is not something new to this generation. Many have been, and continue to be, enamored and encouraged by many godly witnesses from the past. This is not wrong! What makes it so exciting to read of these men of the past is their extreme commitment to the Lord in their personal devotion, their ministry, and their zeal for the Lord. But to try and walk in this same radical discipleship can leave a modern-day believer in the throes of legalism, self-effort, and pride! Where, then, can the balance be found?

One area that I now consider safe to follow after any past hero of the faith is in their personal devotion and relationship to Jesus

Christ. Each of these men knew God. They spent much time with God. The reason I put our thoughts in this direction is that from personal devotion and walking with God comes our callings and gifts. That is the place where God calls us into his purpose and will for our lives.

It is sad to hear stories of young believers who are ministry-minded and full of great zeal for their Lord who read biographies of past saints and then start to emulate their doctrines, style and passion in an exacting way. The sad part is not that they benefit from the example in the Lord they are emulating, but that some of them burn out and even walk away from the faith. Many fall into the trap of championing the exact theology of a saint from the past, which can have errors and imbalances, and then they perpetuate these problems into the modern Christian world. Such believers are sadly being guided more by their zeal and reading of past saints than by their personal walk with the Lord and the guidance of the Spirit of God in their lives.

Some read biographies of famous Christians to try to short-cut themselves into a deeper walk with the Lord and successful ministry. They think: "If I just copy some of their techniques, beliefs, and quotes, I will have their success." Such thinking, though, creates men who trust in the past work of other believers, living out of their zeal instead of tapping into the actual power of God which these men had. True men of God are only signposts to point the way. Their sign should point to heaven, to the Lord himself. The need is for each believer himself to trust in the abiding work of the Holy Spirit. Each of the men covered in this book, who were so mightily used of God, had their faces alight with the glory of God. They saw him. May we not make the mistake of looking to the glory of God on the faces of these men, but rather also set our gaze upward to the actual Lord who will also do the same for us.

It is my prayer for you, as you read through these stirring testimonies and quotes and learn lessons from these godly men of the past, that you also will be become a burning and shining witness in this generation. The abundance is always from him. He is the source of power for the Christian testimony. Our faith must be in God alone. God is calling out today for those who will look to him to be their strength and follow his will. Will you hear the voice of God today and answer the call?

Follow us along on the journey through the lives of these four men who did.

George Whitefield

CHAPTER 1

Pen Sketch of George Whitefield

The name of George Whitefield brings comparatively little recognition in our day, yet in heaven this man is well known! He was a humble servant amongst men but a giant with God. By the age of twenty-one he was the most well-known preacher in all of England. But by the age of twenty-two he was the most hated. He truly is of those "of whom the world was not worthy" (Heb. 11:38), and he was treated thus by the world.

Whitefield was born in Gloucester in 1714. At eighteen he entered Pembroke College, Oxford, and soon became a member of a religious group that included John Wesley and Charles Wesley. The group became known as the Holy Club, or the Oxford Methodists.

Ceasing from Works and Believing Christ

During this time of legalism and striving in a works-based salvation, he worked his body to ill health with fasting and was confined to his bed. Amazingly, it was during this time of rest and recuperation that he was finally changed. He kept simple devotions as his strength allowed. He began to pray simply, and dropped all of his own ideas and efforts and began to really listen to God. At one point he simply threw himself on the bed and cried out, "I thirst!" It was perhaps the first time he had called out to God in utter helplessness. And it was the first time in over a year that he felt happy. At this moment of total surrender to almighty God a new thought now came to his heart, "George, you have what you asked! You ceased to struggle and simply believed and you were born again!" It was so simple, almost absurdly simple, to be saved by such a simple prayer, that it made Whitefield laugh. And as soon as he laughed, the floodgates of heaven burst and he felt "joy, joy unspeakable, joy that's full of, big with glory!" Such a revelation is needed, sadly, in many churches in the world today, where many are keeping rules and strict disciplines to merit eternal salvation. Yet the testimony of the Bible simply states that we are to believe by faith in the work of Christ.

> *For it is by grace you have been saved, through faith—and this is not from yourselves, it is the gift of God* (Eph. 2:8).

And it is Christ's death that saves us from our sins.

> *But God demonstrates his own love for us in this: While we were still sinners, Christ died for us* (Rom. 5:8).

A Nation Turned Upside Down

Whitefield's devotional practice as a youth would be to read a passage of the Bible in English, then in Greek, and then read Matthew Henry's commentary. He would pray over each line he read from these three books until he received it and understood it and it became a part of him. He returned to Gloucester, and during this one year of ministry at the age of twenty-one, the nation of England was stirred and was in an uproar. News spread of his preaching, and thousands came to hear! "Ye must be born again" (John 3:7) was the message that was being trumpeted. When Charles Wesley returned from the mission field he declared, "the whole nation is in an uproar."[1] Another said, "All London and the whole nation ring of the great things of God done by his ministry."[2]

---

1. Kenneth G. C. Newport, *The Letters of Charles Wesley: A Critical Edition, with Introduction and Notes* (Oxford: Oxford University Press, 2013), 66.

2. John Brown, *Memoirs of the Life and Character of the Late Rev. James Hervey* (London: J. & C. Muirhead, 1822), 351.

C. H. Spurgeon said: "It was a brave day for England when Whitefield began field-preaching."[3] With such preaching as this, no wonder the nation was stirred:

> "You must be converted or be damned, and that is plain English; but not plainer than my Master made use of: 'He that believeth not shall be damned.' I did not speak that word strong enough that says, 'He that believeth not shall be damned.' That is the language of our Lord; and it is said of one of the primitive preachers that he used to speak the word 'damned' so that it struck all his auditory."[4]

Whitefield ministered out of a simple full surrender to Jesus Christ, where he fully believed the Bible as the truth; and the greatest reality was what he read in that book. Therefore when he preached, he preached with a sincere faith that was fully persuaded of the truth.

Pleading with Tears for Souls

Here is an example of Whitefield pleading with souls to come to Christ. It is no wonder that there were results, for his preaching moved men because of his broken heart over their lost condition. He was not trying to add members to a church or get converts to report on a denominational stats list; he pleaded with men as if they were the most dearly loved people in the world. The apostle Paul had the same travail from the Lord:

> *I have great sorrow and unceasing anguish in my heart. For I could wish that I myself were cursed and cut off from Christ for the sake of my people, those of my own race* (Rom. 9:2–3).

Whitefield's pleadings were mingled with sobs and tears, for he shared the compassion of his Lord for lost people just as Paul the apostle did earlier:

---

3. Warren W. Wiersbe, *50 People Every Christian Should Know: Learning from Spiritual Giants of the Faith* (Grand Rapids: Baker Books, 2009), 41.

4. George Whitefield, "Repentance and Conversion," accessed June 26, 2014, http://www.gotothebible.com/HTML/Sermons/conversion.html.

I offer you salvation this day. The door of mercy is not yet shut. There does yet remain a sacrifice for sin for all that will accept of the Lord Jesus Christ. He will embrace you in the arms of his love. O turn to him, turn in a sense of your own unworthiness; tell him how polluted you are, how vile, and be not faithless but believing. Why fear ye that the Lord Jesus Christ will not accept of you? Your sins will be no hindrance, your unworthiness no hindrance. If your own corrupt hearts do not keep you back, nothing will hinder Christ from receiving of you. He loves to see poor sinners coming to him. He is pleased to see them lie at his feet pleading his promises; and if you thus come to Christ, he will not send you away without his Spirit; no, but will receive and bless you. O do not put a slight on infinite love—he only wants you to believe on him, that you might be saved. This, this is all the dear Savior desires, to make you happy, that you may leave your sins, to sit down eternally with him at the marriage supper of the Lamb. Let me beseech you to come to Jesus Christ. I invite you all to come to him and receive him as your Lord and Savior. He is ready to receive you. I invite you to come to him, that you may find rest for your souls...

He will rejoice and be glad. He calls you by his ministers. O come unto him—he is laboring to bring you back from sin and from Satan, unto himself; open the door of your hearts and the King of glory shall enter in. My heart is full, it is quite full, and I must speak, or I shall burst. What, do you think your souls of no value? Do you esteem them as not worth saving? Are your pleasures worth more than your souls? Had you rather regard the diversions of this life than the salvation of your souls? If so, you will never be partakers with him in glory; but if you come unto him, he will supply you with his grace here, and bring you to glory hereafter; and there you may sing praises and hallelujahs to the Lamb for ever. And may this be the happy end of all who hear me!"[1]

Cornelius Winter said of Whitefield's preaching: "He seldom, if ever, got through a sermon without tears."[2]

---

1. George Whitefield, "The Folly and Danger of Parting with Christ for the Pleasures and Profits of Life," accessed June 26, 2014, http://tdl.org/txlor-dspace/bitstream/handle/2249.3/725/transcriptwhitefield.htm.

2. Leonard Ravenhill, "George Whitefield: Portrait of a Revival Preacher," accessed June 26, 2014, http://www.ravenhill.org/whitefield.htm.

The Gift of Preaching Used Greatly

Whitefield preached to Presbyterians, Congregationalists, Episcopalians, Catholics, Quakers, and Moravians. He was the first man to so clearly cut across all denominational barriers in his day by preaching the simple truth of the gospel. Whitefield preached more than 18,000 sermons between 1736 and 1770. That is more than ten sermons a week over a period of thirty-four years.

Leonard Ravenhill remarks of Whitefield:

"From a lordly chamber heavy with the pungent aroma of costly perfumes, Whitefield would race off to a street meeting. Catch his joy as he says, 'There I was honored with having stones, dirt, rotten eggs, and pieces of dead cats thrown at me.' What was the secret of Whitefield's success? I think three things: he preached a pure gospel; he preached a powerful gospel; he preached a passionate gospel. He preached to crowds of 30,000 to 78,000 and doing this with no voice amplification of any kind. Whitefield would preach until he literally coughed up blood, and with the warnings of doctors he continued on! He lived in light of eternity continually, and was used of God in this measure."[3]

The Death of this Apostolic Preacher

Whitefield's last letter was dated September 23, 1770. He told how he could not preach, although thousands were waiting to hear. On September 29, he went from Portsmouth, New Hampshire, to Newburyport, Massachusetts. He preached en route in the open at Exeter, New Hampshire. Looking up, he prayed: "Lord Jesus, I am weary in thy work, but not of thy work. If I have not yet finished my course, let me go and speak for thee once more in the fields, seal thy truth, and come home and die." He was given strength for this, his last sermon. The subject was faith and works. Although scarcely able to stand when he first came before the group, he preached for two hours to a crowd that no building then could have held. Arriving at the parsonage of the First Presbyterian Church in Newburyport, a church

3. Ibid.

that he had helped to found, he had supper with his friend, Rev. Jonathan Parsons. He intended to go at once to bed. However, having heard of his arrival, a great number of friends gathered at the parsonage and begged him for just a short message. He paused a moment on the stairs, candle in hand, and spoke to the people as they stood listening until the candle went out. At 2:00 a.m., panting to breathe, he told his traveling companion, Richard Smith: "My asthma is returning; I must have two or three days' rest."[1] His last words were, "I am dying,"[2] and at 6:00 a.m. on Sunday morning, September 30, 1770, he died. The funeral was held on October 2 at the Old South First Presbyterian Church. Thousands of people were unable to even get near the door of the church. Whitefield had requested earlier to be buried beneath the pulpit if he died in that vicinity, which was done. Memorial services were held for him in many places. John Wesley said: "Oh, what has the church suffered in the setting of that bright star which shone so gloriously in our hemisphere. We have none left to succeed him; none of his gifts; none anything like him in usefulness."[3]

It seems rare in church history that God raises up a man of God with the stature of the apostle Paul, George Whitefield, and others, in their train and usefulness with God. Yet we must realize that the gifting of preaching to proclaim and herald the gospel, such as was done by Whitefield, is from God. The body of Christ is full of gifts and callings, and we must also be content with where the Lord has us. But may God raise up others with this gifting and desire for it. Yet may these not only have a loud, authoritative voice, but a deep love for Christ, and love and tears for others.

---

1. Luke Tyerman, *The Life of the Rev. George Whitefield*, Volume 2 (New York: Anson D.F. Randoplh & Company, 1877), 598.

2. Ibid.

3. Susan Martins Miller, *George Whitefield: Clergyman and Scholar* (East Bridgewater: Chelsea House Publishers, 2001), 68.

If I have the gift of prophecy and can fathom all mysteries and all knowl-edge, and if I have a faith that can move mountains, but do not have love, I am nothing (1 Cor. 13:2).

Many more things could be written of this man of God, but we will end with the words of George Whitefield before a large open-air congregation: "At the day of judgment we shall all meet again!"[4]

---

4. Edward and Charles Dilly, *The Works of the Reverend George Whitefield*: Volume 5 (Edinburgh: Kincaid and Bell, 1772), 139.

CHAPTER 2

Lessons Learned from the Life of George Whitefield

What can we gather from the life of George Whitefield for our edification and encouragement today? Many preachers have been and continue to be encouraged by the life of Whitefield, and we also believe his life had many wonderful examples for us to look at as children of God and believers in Jesus Christ. This is not an exhaustive listing of lessons and truths, but only a few helpful ones that we can apply to our Christian lives today.

Lesson 1: Not Seeking the Applause of this World

The first lesson we can learn is that Whitefield fought against the desire to be accepted by the world and its ways. He was esteemed by the masses at age twenty-one and by age twenty-two hated by most. Such is the fickleness of the world we live in and that crucified our Lord. At one moment they want to make him King and at the next moment they are crying out, "Crucify him! Crucify him!" (Luke 23:21).

This world is at enmity with God; and when a god is shown to them that approves of the world-system and their actions, there is an embracing of this god of only benevolent love. Yet when God is shown to be the holy God that cannot stand in the presence of sin, that exposes the sins of the heart, at that moment the hatred of the world becomes utmost. It was in the height of hatred when they crucified God's Son.

This man was handed over to you by God's deliberate plan and fore-knowledge; and you, with the help of wicked men, put him to death by nailing him to the cross. But God raised him from the dead, freeing him from the agony of death, because it was impossible for death to keep its hold on him (Acts 2:23–24).

Therefore let all Israel be assured of this: God has made this Jesus, whom you crucified, both Lord and Messiah (Acts 2:36).

The world-system nailed God himself to a cross and with glee said to themselves: "We have rid him from this earth." They felt now they were safe to continue their wicked ways without them being exposed as evil. As believers, we cannot seek unity with such a world.

We can learn from the life of Whitefield to not seek the favor of the crowds, but to proclaim the truth as God shows it to us, whether that makes us famous or unpopular. Sadly, the applause and favor of the world is something that many modern-day Christians seek after. We want to be radical believers but at the same time be accepted by all others. If our very Lord, who bought us with his blood, was not accepted by this world, should we not consider that it will be the same for us? Whitefield, though he spoke with presidents and kings, still preached the uncompromised gospel of Jesus Christ.

Let us make this practical for all who are reading this. What opportunities do you have in your business, vocation, or school where you can simply follow God's guidance and not make decisions from the pressure of what others will think. Can you, as Whitefield did, speak to men in light that God is watching and knows the intentions of your heart? Will you be willing to speak of sin, or show you do not agree with all the sins that the world enjoys? Simply put, if you can enjoy all the TV shows, movies, and entertainment that the world sells to the masses, then you are enjoying sin and not exposing it. The world will not applaud you if you are not willing to enjoy all its toys, for by doing so you are saying those ways are mingled with sin.

Lesson 2: Thirsting after God

Through the time of legalism and self-effort, Whitefield felt apart from the refreshing, empowering presence of God. His cry, "I thirst!" brought true trust in Christ to him, and he found solace in the very presence of God. This thirsting after God is something we can learn from Whitefield. He would spend days in prayer and prostrate himself on the floor. Why did he do this? Was it for a sermon or a new book? No! He sought God for God himself. He wanted to know God. He saw the great value of the blood of Jesus Christ, and out of great love for God prayed to God intensely.

> *Splendor and majesty are before him; strength and joy are in his dwelling place* (1 Chron. 16:27).

> *As the deer pants for streams of water, so my soul pants for you, my God. My soul thirsts for God, for the living God. When can I go and meet with God?* (Psa. 42:1–2).

How do you feel in your Christian life? Are you tired and worn out by intense schedules, self-effort, and business as usual? Have you sought God in a way that left you satisfied, full of grace and his presence? Whitefield sought God and found him. He found peace and stillness in the presence of an all-sufficient God. The same Godhead is available to us. The Father in heaven is waiting to spend time with us. The way has been opened by the blood of Christ. Free access to seek God and be in his presence has been made. No matter what God has called you to in this life, it will be impossible to fulfill that purpose without having a thirst to seek God in prayer. Thirst means that there is life! Without spiritual thirst, the world will deaden anything of the living God in our hearts.

> *On the last and greatest day of the festival, Jesus stood and said in a loud voice, "Let anyone who is thirsty come to me and drink"* (John 7:37).

Though we live hundreds of years after the life of George Whitefield, we can come to the same God he worshiped and simply say to God, "I thirst." Do that now my friend. Find your satisfaction and fullness in him alone and not anything of this world. God will use you, clean you, fill you and call you for his glory.

Lesson 3: Preaching the Simplicity of the Gospel of Christ

Though in modern evangelicalism we have an abuse of the presentation of the free grace of Christ (known as hyper-grace), this should not cause us to stop preaching and offering that salvation as a free gift from above. George Whitefield trumpeted the message of free grace that Jesus Christ became sin for the world. These old preachers used to preach and make sin so dreadful, hell so wicked, and heaven so beautiful that when they offered and preached of Jesus Christ in all his glory men grabbed at this wonderful free gift. Have you ever heard a powerful gospel presentation where Jesus Christ was shown to be the solution and answer, and your heart leaped within you? Has Jesus Christ ever been made to be wonderful in your eyes?

> *At one time we too were foolish, disobedient, deceived and enslaved by all kinds of passions and pleasures. We lived in malice and envy, being hated and hating one another. But when the kindness and love of God our Savior appeared, he saved us, not because of righteous things we had done, but because of his mercy. He saved us through the washing of rebirth and renewal by the Holy Spirit* (Titus 3:3–5).

Whitefield's message was: "Ye must be born again." Should that not be ours also? Never lose faith in the simple message of trust in the person of Jesus Christ for eternal salvation. In modern America, false professions of faith in Christ are abundant, and many have been made to believe they are saved when they are not. Yet even in that atmosphere we must preach Christ! He is the only solution for the sins of mankind. He is the door to eternal life. Without him we are lost and heading towards an eternal hell. Whitefield preached this message until his dying day. Is that our passion? Is Christ truly that wonderful answer to everything, or is our message different?

Lesson 4: Weeping for Lost Souls

I can already sense that some readers are being lost in the grandeur of these things. "Surely there is no one alive that is like George Whitefield," someone can think in their doubting mind. Yet we can distill it down more simply thus far. Do you live separate from the world, seek God in prayer beyond other needs, and share the good news of the gospel with others? If so, then you are doing what Whitefield did. You do not need to sound like him or preach to 10,000 people at once—you in your normal simple life working as a newspaper delivery man or plumber, or perhaps a business owner or computer developer. You! Yes, you can do the same things that Whitefield did and share in the same experiences that he has in measure with Jesus Christ.

Why did Whitefield weep so much for souls? He did this publicly in open-air meetings, where the front row of the audience were wet with some of his tears as he passionately proclaimed faith. Whitefield was a passionate preacher, and some accused him of dramatism because of his body movements and emotional language. Yet his tears showed his sincerity. He simply was close enough to God that God shared his burdens with him.

> *Jerusalem, Jerusalem, you who kill the prophets and stone those sent to you, how often I have longed to gather your children together, as a hen gathers her chicks under her wings, and you were not willing* (Matt. 23:37).

> *The Lord is not slow in keeping his promise, as some understand slowness. Instead he is patient with you, not wanting anyone to perish, but everyone to come to repentance* (2 Peter 3:9).

You, my friend, can seek God in your own life and come close enough to him where he will start to break your heart over men and women that do not know him. It may be that poor starving child you see in humanitarian ads. But if you are sharing God's true heart, you will start to see normal people in society as sad, broken, lost ones who are eternally apart from God.

Would you pray to the Lord to have him share his broken heart for the lost? Christ still is weeping over this broken world of seven billion souls. Just as in the days of Noah, God's heart breaks. God is love. He desires none to perish. Life is a breath. Eternity is soon. Whitefield saw it and wept.

CHAPTER 3

Inspiring Quotes from George Whitefield

George Whitefield's name is known in modern evangelism primarily through the shorthand sermons that were passed on and published, through his personal journal, and through numerous biographies and historical accounts of his first great awakening. He was a man of one passion: to glorify Jesus Christ in evangelistic preaching. His was the gospel to proclaim; he could do no other. Whitefield wrote in his journal: "I was honored today with having a few stones, dirt, rotten eggs, and pieces of dead cat thrown at me."[1] May we in our day honor this man of God by learning something from his passion, zeal, and willingness to suffer for the Lord.

J. C. Ryle wrote of the lack of written materials by or about Whitefield:

"The materials for forming a correct opinion about such a man as Whitefield are necessarily very scanty. He wrote no book for the millions, of world-wide fame, like Bunyan's *Pilgrim's Progress*. He headed no crusade against an apostate church, with a nation at his back and princes on his side, like Martin Luther. He founded no religious denomination which pinned its faith on his writings and carefully embalmed his best acts and words, like John Wesley. There are Lutherans and Wesleyans in the present day, but there are no Whitefieldites. No! The great evangelist ... was a simple, guileless man who lived for one thing only, and that was to preach Christ. If he did that, he cared for nothing else. The records of such a man

---

1. Alvin Reid, *Evangelism Handbook: Biblical, Spiritual, Intentional, Missional* (Nashville: B&H Publishing Group, 2009), 202.

are large and full in heaven I have no doubt, but they are few and scanty upon earth."[1]

Quotes from George Whitefield

The Christian world is in a deep sleep; nothing but a loud shout can awaken them out of it!

If your souls were not immortal, and you in danger of losing them, I would not thus speak unto you; but the love of your souls constrains me to speak: methinks this would constrain me to speak unto you forever.

It is an undoubted truth that every doctrine that comes from God leads to God; and that which doth not tend to promote holiness is not of God.

I believe I never was more acceptable to my master than when I was standing to teach those hearers in the open fields. I now preach to ten times more people than I would if I had been confined to the churches.

What! Get to heaven on your own strength? Why, you might as well try to climb to the moon on a rope of sand!

Oh that I was lowly in heart! Honor and dishonor, good report and evil report would then be alike, and prove a furtherance to me in my Christian cause.

True conversion means turning not only from sin but also from depending on self-made righteousness. Those who trust in their own righteousness for conversion hide behind their own good works. This is the reason that self-righteous people are so angry with gospel preachers, because the gospel does not spare those who will not submit to the righteousness of Jesus Christ!

A true faith in Jesus Christ will not suffer us to be idle. No, it is an active, lively, restless principle; it fills the heart, so that it cannot be easy till it is doing something for Jesus Christ.

---

1. J. C. Ryle, *The Christian Leaders of the Last Century: Or England a Hundred Years Ago* (Edinburgh: T. Nelson and Sons, 1869), 44.

The great and important duty which is incumbent on Christians is to guard against all appearance of evil; to watch against the first risings in the heart to evil; and to have a guard upon our actions, that they may not be sinful, or so much as seem to be so.

There is not a thing on the face of the earth that I abhor so much as idleness or idle people.

How sweet is rest after fatigue! How sweet will heaven be when our journey is ended.

If one evil thought, if one evil word, if one evil action, deserves eternal damnation, how many hells, my friends, do every one of us deserve, whose whole lives have been one continued rebellion against God!

At the day of judgment we shall all meet again.

The care of the soul is "a matter of the highest importance," beyond anything which can be brought into comparison with it.

But he is unworthy the name of a minister of the gospel of peace who is unwilling, not only to have his name cast out as evil, but also to die for the truths of the Lord Jesus.

Press forward. Do not stop, do not linger in your journey, but strive for the mark set before you.

The Lord Jesus Christ, when he first comes to you, finds you full of sin and pollution; you are deformed, defiled, enslaved, poor, miserable and wretched, very despicable and loathsome, by reason of sin; and he maketh choice of you, not because of your holiness, nor of your beauty, nor of your being qualified for them; no, the Lord Jesus Christ puts these qualifications upon you, as may make you meet for his embrace; and you are drawn to make choice of the Lord Jesus Christ because he first chose you.

Whole days and weeks have I spent prostrate on the ground in silent or vocal prayer.

The reason why congregations have been so dead is because they have dead men preaching to them. How can dead men beget living children?

We are immortal till our work is done.

It is a poor sermon that gives no offense—that neither makes the hearer displeased with himself nor with the preacher.

God forbid that I should travel with anybody a quarter of an hour without speaking of Christ to them.

The riches of his free grace cause me daily to triumph over all the temptations of the wicked one, who is very vigilant, and seeks all occasions to disturb me.

O my brethren, my heart is enlarged towards you. I trust I feel something of that hidden but powerful presence of Christ whilst I am preaching to you.

And now let me address all of you, high and low, rich and poor, one with another, to accept of mercy and grace while it is offered to you. Now is the accepted time, now is the day of salvation; and will you not accept it, now it is offered unto you?

God has condescended to become an author, and yet people will not read his writings. There are very few that ever gave this Book of God, the grand charter of salvation, one fair reading through.

Go to bed seasonably, and rise early. Redeem your precious time. Pick up the fragments of it, that not one moment of it may be lost. Be much in secret prayer. Converse less with man and more with God.

Venture daily upon Christ, go out in his strength, and he will enable you to do wonders.

Be content with no degree of sanctification. Be always crying out, "Lord, let me know more of myself and of thee."

Gladly shall I come whenever bodily strength will allow to join my testimony with yours in Olney pulpit, that God is love. As yet I have not recovered from the fatigues of my American expedition. My shattered bark is scarce worth docking any more. But I would fain wear, not rust, out. Oh! my dear Mr. Newton, indeed and indeed I am ashamed that I have done and suffered so little for him that hath done and suffered so much for ill and hell-deserving me.

If I see a man who loves the Lord Jesus in sincerity, I am not very solicitous to what communion he belongs. The kingdom of God, I think, does not consist in any such thing.

Come, come unto him. If your souls were not immortal, and you in danger of losing them, I would not thus speak unto you; but the love of your souls constrains me to speak. Methinks this would constrain me to speak unto you forever. Come then by faith and lay hold of the Lord Jesus; though he be in heaven, he now calleth thee. Come, all ye drunkards, swearers, Sabbath-breakers, adulterers, fornicators; come, all ye scoffers, harlots, thieves, and murderers, and Jesus Christ will save you; he will give you rest, if you are weary of your sins. O come lay hold upon him. Had I less love for your souls, I might speak less; but that love of God, which is shed abroad in my heart, will not permit me to leave you till I see whether you will come to Christ or no. O for your life receive him, for fear he may never call you any more. Behold, the Bridegroom cometh; it may be this night the cry may be made. Now would you hear this, if you were sure to die before the morning light? God grant you may begin to live, that when the king of terrors shall come, you may have nothing to do but to commit your souls into the hands of a faithful Redeemer.

John Cennick

Chapter 4

Pen Sketch of John Cennick

John Cennick was punched in the nose, beaten until his shoulders were black and blue, dunked in a dirty pond, sprayed with ditch water, and blackened with musket smoke when he preached. Hecklers tried to drown his voice by beating drums and pans. Or they set dogs barking by swinging a cat in a cage. They hurled dead dogs at him. In spite of this terrible opposition, he preached outdoor sermons in Wiltshire for five years. He wanted to win souls.[1]

Does that sound like a fictional story or something unbelievable? Yet it is the true history of a man of God who lived in England during the 1700s. The apostle John, many years before, warned that the world would be hostile to the Lord's message:

Do not be surprised, my brothers and sisters, if the world hates you (1 John 3:13).

This was a true reality for Cennick every day as he preached the good news of Christ and shared the light of the gospel with those who were in darkness. We think of England as a wonderful Christian country, but in those days there was vehement opposition to the truths of God's Word.

A God-Filled Man

In the life of the church we run across men of such stature that they seem to tower over the masses of professed believers. John Cennick was used of God in such proportions that can only be

---

1. Dan Graves, "Young John Cennick Out of His Head with Fever," accessed June 27, 2014, http://www.christianity.com/church/church-history/timeline/1701-1800/young-john-cennick-out-of-his-head-with-fever-11630261.html.

labeled as apostolic! He was a God-filled man with a God-filled message. And such a filling of God's Spirit is 100 percent open to all of us that desire to be used of him:

> *But you will receive power when the Holy Spirit comes on you; and you will be my witnesses in Jerusalem, and in all Judea and Samaria, and to the ends of the earth* (Acts 1:8).

He preached "Christ crucified" (1 Cor. 1:23) and did not stop sharing the Scriptures with crowds that opposed him, even when demanded. He labored amongst the Methodists, Calvinists, and finally amongst the Moravians. He was not a "denominational man" but rather was a "God appointed man" who did not shrink back from declaring the whole counsel of God. Do we not need such men who will fear God more than men?

> *But I will show you whom you should fear: Fear him who, after your body has been killed, has authority to throw you into hell. Yes, I tell you, fear him* (Luke 12:5).

Who will suffer for the preaching of the everlasting gospel, and who will belong to God above all human ties?

> *Therefore, since Christ suffered in his body, arm yourselves also with the same attitude, because whoever suffers in the body is done with sin* (1 Peter 4:1).

> *So, my brothers and sisters, you also died to the law through the body of Christ, that you might belong to another, to him who was raised from the dead, in order that we might bear fruit for God* (Rom. 7:4).

Desiring to be Bold as a Lion

At nine years of age, he heard his dying aunt exclaim, "Last night the Lord stood by me and invited me to drink of the fountain of life freely, and I shall stand before the Lord as bold as a lion." For years John was unable to get those words out of his head. What a privilege to be able to stand before the Lord as bold as a lion! How he wished he could be sure of the same future. He prayed, fasted, hoped for it, but found himself unable to do good. He lied and cheated and frittered his hours in spite of his best resolutions to do otherwise. One day, his heart became unbearably heavy. He entered a church to pray. As he knelt there, he seemed to hear Jesus say, "I am your salvation." The weight rolled off him. His desires changed. No longer did he want to fritter his time on cards. One day when he refused to play for the sake of his conscience, he was told that there was another "stupid religious fellow" like himself. The man turned out to be a Methodist who introduced John Cennick to John Wesley. Soon John Cennick was standing under a tree in Kingswood, preaching for the Methodists.[1]

John Cennick would become one of the most outstanding preachers of the eighteenth century revival. Known as the "Apostle of Wiltshire," because of his early evangelistic work in that county, his most important legacy was his preaching in Ireland.[2]

Born of Quaker parents, raised in the Anglican Church, he joined the Methodist movement. But after several years with the Wesleyan Methodists, he broke with John Wesley and joined George Whitefield's Calvinistic Methodists. Later he left the Calvinistic Methodists for the Moravian Brethren. When clergymen complained that their churches were empty because everyone had gone to hear John, Bishop Rider replied, "Preach Christ crucified and then the people will not have to go to Cennick to hear the gospel."[3] There is need in our day of such men who will be simply led where God wants them and not have allegiances to build denominations only; for the true work of the gospel is to build God's kingdom and see it come to earth as it is in heaven.

Great Crowds and Great Suffering

Cennick preached twice daily to crowds so great that those who wished to hear must be present two or three hours before the time. All the windows were taken down so that people might hear in the

1. Ibid.

2. Faith Cook, "Triumphs of grace," accessed June 27, 2014, http://www.evangelical-times.org/archive/item/63/Historical/Triumphs-of-grace.

3. J. E. Hutton, "History of the Moravian Church, Chapter 11," accessed June 27, 2014, http://www.ccel.org/ccel/hutton/moravian.v.xi.html

burying-ground, yard, and environs, yet multitudes were disappoint-ed. On Sundays all the tops of the houses near the meeting house, all walls and windows were covered with people, and Cennick had to go in at the window, creeping over the heads of the people to reach his pulpit. Often seven or eight priests were together to hear him, and many of the church clergy, many teachers of religion and many collegians.[1]

What an amazing scene almost beyond imagination. May God raise up such an interest and desire for the Word of God in our day that we would clamor to hear it even with a cost involved.

In another account we hear of his hard labors for Christ: "He ranged out over seven counties in Ireland, holding meetings in barns or fields or houses, preaching every day and often several times a day, and forming Moravian Societies. He was beaten by hoodlums, attacked by mobs, set upon by dogs, and was arrested and fined. He and his wife lived in poverty, yet were often over-flowing with the joy of the Lord. He condemned sin in every form and was utterly uncompromising in his gospel declaration."

We hear again another account of the hard, laborious trials he endured: "Cennick often addressed thousands in the open air, with rain coming down in torrents. He preached in old barns, disused cloth mills, and in village cock-pits. He slept in the old ruined church at Portmore. He sat on the roadside, cold and lonely, munching his meager lunch of bread and cheese. If money was plentiful, he used a horse; if not, he would walk twenty miles to preach."

We have to realize that true Christians have suffered much for the spreading of the message we believe today. It was with a great cost that from the twelve disciples that Jesus taught, we now have over one billion possible believers in Jesus Christ. It only came by one way: suffering!

---

1. Arnold A. Dallimore, *George Whitefield: God's Anointed Servant in the Great Revival of the Eighteenth Century* (Wheaton, Crossway Books, 1990), 176.

Now if we are children, then we are heirs—heirs of God and co-heirs with Christ, if indeed we share in his sufferings in order that we may also share in his glory (Rom. 8:17).

Apostolic Christianity is Christianity that bears the cross of Christ and follows in the sufferings of Christ.

I will show him how much he must suffer for my name (Acts 9:16).

Cennick followed the path his Master trod and was very familiar with suffering for the name that he counted so precious.

The apostles left the Sanhedrin, rejoicing because they had been counted worthy of suffering disgrace for the name (Acts 5:41).

May God open our hearts to take small steps in suffering for this glorious expansion of the gospel in our day and time.

The Way of Suffering

We have many lessons to learn from this apostolic figure in church history. His life teaches us that suffering is something we must not disdain but embrace. His life also teaches us to have a boldness for sharing the truth of the Bible with a lost and needy world. Why are there no more modern day John Cennicks, you may ask? I would simply reply: when we have a man that will suffer for the gospel as much as Cennick, then we will truly have another John Cennick! These Scriptures must have been close to this man of God's heart:

If you are insulted because of the name of Christ, you are blessed, for the Spirit of glory and of God rests on you (1 Peter 4:14).

However, if you suffer as a Christian, do not be ashamed, but praise God that you bear that name (1 Peter 4:16).

In bringing many sons and daughters to glory, it was fitting that God, for whom and through whom everything exists, should make the pioneer of their salvation perfect through what he suffered (Heb. 2:10).

John Cennick's life ended abruptly as he passed away in England, after having a fever for five days. He died at the age of thirty six! By the time of his early death, he had established over forty churches. Matthew Wilks said of Cennick: "His Christian qualities were not less distinguishable. If unaffected humility, deadness to the world, a life of communion with God, and a cheerful reliance on a crucified Savior constitute the real Christian, he was one of an eminent degree. 'Tis true, his language was not with the enticing words of man's wisdom; yet his doctrine and address were powerful, and found access to the hearts of thousands."[1] George Whitefield remarked upon hearing of the death of Cennick: "John Cennick is now added to the happy number of those who are called to see God as he is!"[2] And with the same faith may we all realize that we see God in a mirror dimly, but let us pursue the relationship with our heavenly Father and simply obey his voice to us. God might not call us to do such radical things as Cennick, but if we just follow the will of God for each of our own lives as simple slaves of Christ we will be pleasing to our Father in heaven.

1. John Holmes, *History of the Protestant Church of the United Brethren*, Volume 1 (Edinburgh: J. Nisbet, 1825), 336.

2. Luke Tyerman, *The Life of the Rev. George Whitefield*, Volume 2 (New York: Anson D. F. Randolph, 1877), 345–346.

CHAPTER 5

Lessons Learned from the Life of John Cennick

John Cennick's life story is another powerful testimony of a brother from the past who walked in utter obedience to his heavenly Master. What can we learn from such a one that suffered so much? Perhaps some with the modern Western mind will consider one that suffered so much of little value to us because the way of the cross is not something even considered biblical by some modern believers. Viewed by those who hold to a theology that exalts prosperity, healing, and personal success in this world, Cennick's life was hardly "Your Best Life Now,"[3] but rather it was a best life later! He was laboring in light of eternity. Let us look at some short lessons from his life to help us forward in our walks with the Lord today.

Lesson 1: Suffering for Jesus Christ

Have you ever been hit by someone because you believed in Jesus Christ? Beaten? Probably not. Such has been the lot of many godly men in the past; and even today martyrdoms for the sake of Christ and the gospel are rapidly increasing. Today there are more people martyred for the faith of Christ than ever before in history. It is estimated that every year over 150,000 people in the world are martyred for the Christian faith.[4]

---

3. Joel Osteen, *Your Best Life Now: 7 Steps to Living at Your Full Potential* (New York, FaithWords, 2007).

4. Art Babych, "Christianity: the Most Persecuted World Faith," accessed June 27, 2014, http://www.saintanthonyofpadua.net/messaggero/pagina_stampa.asp?R=&ID=118.

Now in comparison to this, how do we suffer? Cennick suffered much, including the deriding of his name and reputation. Perhaps that comes a bit closer to home for us. Have you ever had someone speak ill of you because you shared with them that you are a Christian? Now we can see how we can suffer in the same way as Cennick did in his day. But just to suffer for Christ is not the lesson that we intend to learn here, but rather *how* he suffered.

"They hurled dead dogs at him." Do you suppose he threw those dogs back at them? His response was rather one of humility and love. He endured all the evil that men did to him because in his mind he knew that the Savior he preached suffered the same things from men. He took seriously the admonition of the apostle Peter:

> *Therefore, since Christ suffered in his body, arm yourselves also with the same attitude, because whoever suffers in the body is done with sin* (1 Peter 4:1).

And our Lord speaks to those who will bear reproach for his name:

> *Blessed are you when people insult you, persecute you and falsely say all kinds of evil against you because of me* (Matt. 5:11).

> *But I tell you, love your enemies and pray for those who persecute you, that you may be children of your Father in heaven. He causes his sun to rise on the evil and the good, and sends rain on the righteous and the unrighteous* (Matt. 5:44–45).

May we, as Cennick did, suffer gracefully and be uncompromising in our faith as we stand for our Lord, even in the midst of trials and suffering from men.

Lesson 2: Being Filled with the Holy Spirit

Cennick was, to those who saw him, a markedly different man. He seemed different. There was something about him that spoke of heaven. Others labeled him "apostolic," sensing something of the genuine early church Christianity in him. I would rather in our day speak of him as a man filled with the Holy Spirit. How did the early apostles choose servants for the work of the church? We find this written in the book of Acts:

> *Brothers and sisters, choose seven men from among you who are known to be full of the Spirit and wisdom. We will turn this responsibility over to them* (Acts 6:3).

Therefore we see that the early apostles were able to discern by noticing the life of men around them who were full of the Spirit. In another place in the book of Acts this same Stephen, when being brought before the council of religious Jews and being persecuted, his countenance was noticeably different than others:

> *All who were sitting in the Sanhedrin looked intently at Stephen, and they saw that his face was like the face of an angel* (Acts 6:15).

So we see from these passages that there can be something noticeably different in a person who is filled with the living God. Cennick was such a man. Another mark of being full of the Holy Spirit is boldness. John Cennick did not relent in his preaching of the good news of Jesus Christ amidst great opposition, thus verifying a power at work in him to be uncompromising in his generation. The lesson and blessing for us is the same: Holy Spirit baptism is available to us today. The filling of the Spirit of God is a gift from God, so it is available to any believer of Jesus Christ who desires it. We must sense our great need before God, and have a desperation for this empowering from above.

> *For John baptized with water, but in a few days you will be baptized with the Holy Spirit* (Acts 1:5).

> *Which of you fathers, if your son asks for a fish, will give him a snake instead? Or if he asks for an egg, will give him a scorpion? If you then, though you are evil, know how to give good gifts to your children, how much more will your Father in heaven give the Holy Spirit to those who ask him!* (Luke 11:11–13).

Friend, call out to God today. He will give you what you need to be a bold witness for him, just as he did with godly Cennick many years ago.

Lesson 3: Working for God, not Men

Cennick saw himself primarily as God's worker and not working for men. He worked amongst three different large movements in his day but saw it much more important to be simply following the Lord himself. He was faithful in every assignment and did not speak against other groups. Also, his theology changed throughout his life and he was teachable and open to correction by God, "preaching every day and often several times a day, and forming Moravian Societies." He ended up until his death laboring with the Moravian movement, which in his day was full of great life and power from above. The Moravians were essentially one of the great examples to the rest of Christendom of zeal for missions and trust in the Spirit's power to be witnesses. They testified of the bloodied Lamb of God that came to rescue men by his blood shed for them.

This is a lesson for us to learn: that we must follow the path set out by the Holy Spirit in our lives. Sometimes God will lead us to work with one Christian group for a season and then call us onward to another group or to start a church. This can go against modern reasoning, which says that if you labor with one group long enough you will receive status, experience, and connections. Such is sadly the business mindset that has crept into the church, where there is a sense of a corporate ladder to climb in the church, to receive more benefit as a minister of the gospel. Cennick would not have any of it and simply obeyed and followed his Lord.

In his letter to the Galatians, we can see this same desire in the apostle Paul to simply follow the Lord himself and not men:

> But when God, who set me apart from my mother's womb and called me by his grace, was pleased to reveal his Son in me so that I might preach him among the Gentiles, my immediate response was not to consult any human being. I did not go up to Jerusalem to see those who were apostles before I was, but I went into Arabia. Later I returned to Damascus (Gal. 1:15–17).

Could God be calling you away from the group you are involved in? To be uncompromising in your faith may require it. God is doing a *new thing* in the earth and is always in each generation working apart from many religious systems that have closed themselves off from the life of God. Such was the case in Cennick's day—the Church of England was primarily a state-run religious entity that persecuted the true elect of God. It is the same in our day. Even many mainstream denominations are starting to persecute those who are true to God's Word and gospel.

CHAPTER 6

Inspiring Quotes from John Cennick

Not much has been preserved from the preaching of Cennick. The copies of sermons that have been preserved are rare and hard to find. This could be for a variety of reasons, including his allegiance to the Son of God and not to one specific denomination or movement during his life. Though he was very faithful in laboring with other brethren under authority, he transited between three large movements in his day: the Calvinistic Methodists, the Wesleyan Methodists, and the Moravians. Perhaps no one felt that they owed him, and thus did not preserve many of his writings. Cennick's hymns, though, have stood the test of time; and we include these hymns in quotation form here to see some of his heart for the Lord in writing.[1]

Lo! He cometh

Lo! He cometh, countless trumpets
Blow before his bloody sign!
'Midst ten thousand saints and angels,
See the Crucified shine.
Allelujah!
Welcome, welcome bleeding Lamb!

Thou dear Redeemer

Thou dear Redeemer, dying Lamb,
I love to hear of thee;
No music like thy charming name,
Is half so sweet to me.

---

1. John Cennick Hymns, Cyber Hymnal, accessed June 27, 2014, http://www.cyberhymnal.org/bio/c/e/cennick_j.htm

O let me ever hear thy voice,
In mercy to me speak!
And in my priest, will I rejoice,
My great Melchizedek.

My Jesus shall be still my theme,
While in this world I stay;
I'll sing my Jesus' lovely name,
When all things else decay.

When I appear in yonder cloud,
With all thy favored throng,
Then I will sing more sweet, more loud,
And Christ shall be my song.

Lo, I come

Hosanna, Hosanna, to the Lamb!
Hosanna, Hosanna, to the Lamb!

Lo, I come, and thou, blest Lamb,
Shall take me to thee whose I am.

Hosanna, etc.

Nothing but sin have I to give,
Nothing but love shall I receive.

Hosanna, etc.

Savior and Regenerator

Savior and regenerator!
Thee alone, God we own,
Father and creator.

Word incarnate, we adore thee!
Hosts above, God of love,
Cast their crowns before thee.

Father, Son and Holy Spirit,
One in thee, Lord, we see,
Who thy grace inherit.

May thy Word be our instructor,
Night and day, on our way,
Our divine conductor!

Visit us with thy salvation;
Let thy care still be near,
Round our habitation.

Jesus, our divine protector,
Guide us still, let
Thy will be our sole director!

Lo! He comes with clouds descending

Yea, Amen! Let all adore thee,
High on thine eternal throne;
Savior, take the power and glory,
Claim the kingdom for thine own;
O come quickly! O come quickly! O come quickly!
Everlasting God, come down!

Come, my soul, before the LAMB

Come, my soul, before the LAMB,
Fall and do him reverence!
Bless him for his blood and name,
Sing his great deliverance.

Cast thy burdens on the Lord,
Leave them with thy Savior;
He, whose hands for thee were bor'd.
Can and will deliver.

Children of the heavenly King

Children of the heavenly King,
As ye journey, sweetly sing;
Sing your Savior's worthy praise,
Glorious in his works and ways.

We are traveling home to God,
In the way the fathers trod;
They are happy now, and we
Soon their happiness shall see.

Fear not, brethren; joyful stand.
On the borders of your land;
Jesus Christ, your Father's Son,
Bids you undismayed go on.

Lift your eyes, ye sons of light,
Zion's city is in sight:
There our endless home shall be,
There our Lord in glory see.

Daily us prepare and fit,
On thy holy throne to sit!
More and more adorn thy seed,
Meet to triumph with our head.

Seal our love, our labors end,
Let us to thy bliss ascend;
Let us to thy kingdom come;
Lord, we long to be at home.

Hail, church of Christ

Hail, church of Christ, bought with his blood!
The world I freely leave;
Ye children of the living God,
Me in your tents receive.

Bride of the Lamb! I'm one in heart
With thee, through boundless grace,
And I will never from thee part;
This bond shall never cease.

Closely I'll follow Christ with thee,
I'll go thy safest road;
Thy people shall my people be,
And thine shall be my God.

Lines, by the late Mr. Cennick

Now, Lord, at peace with thee and all below,
Let me depart, and to thy kingdom go.

The doctrine of our dying Lord

The doctrine of our dying Lord,
The faith he on Mount Calvary sealed
We sign, asserting ev'ry word
Which in his gospel is revealed
As truth divine; and cursed are they
Who add thereto or take away.

We steadfastly this truth maintain,
that none is righteous, no not one;
That in the Lamb, for sinners slain,
We're justified by faith alone,
And all who in his name believe.
Christ and his righteousness receive.

George Fox

CHAPTER 7

Pen Sketch of George Fox

George Fox alone has, without human learning, done more than any other reformer in Protestant Christendom towards the restoration of real, primitive, unadulterated Christianity and the destruction of priest craft, superstition, and ridiculous, unavailing rites and ceremonies.　　　　　　　　　　　　　　　—Leonard Ravenhill[1]

Unadulterated Christianity

As an earthquake shakes the earth, bringing keen awareness of its activity, so our subject George Fox quaked with such force that England was made aware of this young firebrand in the hand of the Lord. With not man as his teacher but God, he brought messages to common folk and priests alike. With prophetic force and unction, this man's voice shattered the religious status quo of the day. As Leonard Ravenhill remarks of this man, "Though he made others shake, no man could make him shake." Clothed in a leather suit, boots, and hat, he appeared much like a John the Baptist character to the Church of England professors of religion. In church history we see God raise up prophets to do his will and correct large unbalances that were prevalent in the body of Christ. This spirit of prophecy that was in George Fox was the same voice that corrected the seven churches in Revelation, in some cases very severely.

Here I am! I stand at the door and knock. If anyone hears my voice and opens the door, I will come in and eat with that person, and they with me (Rev. 3:20).

---

1. Leonard Ravenhill, "George Fox—The Unshakable Shaker," accessed June 27, 2014, http://www.ravenhill.org/fox.htm.

In most cases it is very hard to embrace the message these prophets bring. Though even they can be imbalanced at times, they still bring a corrective measure against gross misuse of the Scriptures and of God's authority.

In the beginning of the Journal of George Fox, he gives the reason for writing the accounts of his life: "That all may know the dealings of the Lord with me... to prepare and fit me for the work unto which he had appointed me."[1] George Fox was God-appointed; his calling was by the Spirit of God; his life was wholly given to Christ, the Savior of men's souls. He took no heed to professors, books, and men. Such a spirit was that of the apostle Paul, who stated:

> *Am I now trying to win the approval of human beings, or of God? Or am I trying to please people? If I were still trying to please people, I would not be a servant of Christ* (Gal 1:10–11).

May God raise up more men who know their calling and are able to walk in that authority from God.

> *Paul, an apostle—sent not from men nor by a man, but by Jesus Christ and God the Father, who raised him from the dead* (Gal 1:1).

A Stranger to All

George Fox was born in 1624 and was raised in a religious home in the shoemaker trade. Being keenly aware of the spiritual, he had many experiences of God in his heart, as the Spirit of God was wooing this young man to himself. At the age of nineteen he had familiarity with some Puritans, who one day at a tavern had him to drink. Their worldly actions grieved George Fox to a point of leaving and not being able to sleep that entire night. As he sought the Lord with tears, the Lord spoke to his servant, telling him to forsake all and become a stranger upon the earth. And this he did! Obeying the voice of the Lord, he left his town,

---

1. George Fox, *Journal of George Fox: Being an Historical Account of the Life, Travels and Labour of Love in the Work of the Ministry* (London: W. & F.G. Cash, 1820), 49.

his family, his life, without any notice or farewells. This desperate young man left as Abraham of old left—"and he went out, not knowing whither he went" (Heb. 11:8). As he passed from town to town, professors of religion were keen to speak to this unusual young man; but, as he confesses in his journal, "I was afraid of them, for I was sensible they did not possess what they professed."[2]

For the next few years his time was spent in agony of body and soul, being grieved at the state of religion and men's hearts, even so much that at points in time he wished, in his own words, "…I had never been born."[3] Then came a voice to him as clear as the one that called him from his home: "There is one, even Jesus Christ, that can speak to thy condition," and Fox says: "When I heard it, my heart did leap for joy."

The revival historian David Smithers shares some great insight into this remarkable life: "Soon after George Fox began to preach, he had a remarkable spiritual experience that lasted fourteen days. A certain Mr. Brown, while on his death bed, prophesied many great things concerning Fox."

"When this man was buried," said Fox, "a great work of the Lord fell on me." During this mighty baptism of the Spirit, Fox received a remarkable gift of discernment. "He seemed to be able to read the character of men by looking at them." Miraculous healing also accompanied his ministry. Through prayer and the laying on of hands, the sick were often healed and devils were cast out to the glory of Christ. When George Fox preached, men would shake and tremble. "The name Quaker was given to Fox and his followers, because of the quaking of the men who came to scoff but stayed to pray." This remarkable power seemed to accompany Fox's preaching wherever he went. He preached that Jesus Christ is the author of a faith which purifies and gives victory over sin. He fervently exhorted men to pursue complete

---

2. George Fox, *George Fox—An Autobiography* Chapter 1: Boyhood—A Seeker, accessed June 27, 2014, http://www.strecorsoc.org/gfox/ch01.html.

3. Ibid.

holiness rather than empty religious ceremonies, and often pointed out that what was commonly called the church was only a building. He boldly declared that only the fervent believers of Christ were the living stones of the true church."[1] As a result, he was often beaten, stoned, and driven out of town. He usually went about the country on foot, dressed in his famous suit of leather clothes, which it is believed he made himself. He often slept outside under a tree or in some haystack.

A Free Gospel

God had burdened George Fox to speak to the shepherds of his day who were taking care of the flocks of God's people in England. Fox had a peculiar spiritual gift of being able to discern true and spurious profession, and thus saw that many of the shepherds were just hirelings who were in priest craft for the wages and prominence, and not for love of the body of Christ. He seemed to trumpet this message against the selling of Christ and religion with a burdened and jealous heart, much like Christ himself toppling the moneychangers' tables.

> The worldly spirit of the priests made him suffer; and when he heard the bells ring to call worshipers to the steeple-houses, it struck him to the heart, for it was just like a market-bell to gather people together that the priest might set forth his ware to sale. Oh, the vast sums of money that are gotten by the trade they make of selling the Scriptures, and by their preaching… notwithstanding the Scriptures were given forth freely, and Christ commanded his ministers to preach freely.[2]

Another point that touches at the very heart of George Fox's ministry was telling people that God has come to teach them himself. It is brought out clearly in his journal when he said:

1. David Smithers, "George Fox," accessed June 27, 2014, http://www.watchword.org/index.php?option=com_content&task=view&id=23.

2. Samuel Macpherson Janney, *The life of George Fox; with dissertations on his views concerning the doctrines, testimonies, and discipline of the Christian church*, (Philadelphia: Lippincott, 1853), 46.

"These things I did not see by the help of man, nor by the letter, though they are written in the letter; but I saw them in the light of the Lord Jesus Christ, and by his immediate Spirit and power, as did the holy men of God, by whom the Holy Scriptures were written."[3] In our day there is a sad neglect of authority, and submission to authority, which is strongly commanded in Scripture. Yet such submission and authority must encourage the people of God to come to maturity, so that we can all be taught of God.

Have confidence in your leaders and submit to their authority, because they keep watch over you as those who must give an account. Do this so that their work will be a joy, not a burden, for that would be of no benefit to you (Heb. 13:17).

Until we all reach unity in the faith and in the knowledge of the Son of God and become mature, attaining to the whole measure of the fullness of Christ (Eph. 4:13).

As for you, the anointing you received from him remains in you, and you do not need anyone to teach you. But as his anointing teaches you about all things and as that anointing is real, not counterfeit—just as it has taught you, remain in him (1 John 2:27).

Such a ministry George Fox had to bring people to this "light,"[4] that Christ was in them by his Spirit to teach and grow them into his likeness.

For those God foreknew he also predestined to be conformed to the image of his Son, that he might be the firstborn among many brothers and sisters (Rom. 8:29).

Fox stressed the important truth that in seeking to understand and interpret the Scriptures, we should not set aside the offices of the Holy Spirit, the author of the Scriptures. He felt that many

---

3. George Amoss, "George Fox's Teaching on the Place of Scripture," accessed June 27, 2014, http://www.qis.net/~daruma/foxbible.html.

4. Inner light, from Wikipedia, the free encyclopedia, accessed June 27, 2014, http://en.wikipedia.org/wiki/Inner_light.

in his day were holding steadfastly to the written Word of God, but only as a dead letter. On one occasion he pointed out that "the Jews had the Scriptures, and yet resisted the Holy Ghost, and rejected Christ, the bright morning star." By rejecting the enlightening aid of the Holy Spirit on the written Word, they erred in judgment regarding the identity of God's Son.

Reading and studying the Scriptures is an important part of our lives as Christians, but as Fox emphasized, we must always seek the aid of the Holy Spirit in interpretation and application and not allow God's Word to become a dead letter, leading to a dead orthodoxy instead of a living faith.

Holy Men's Words

George Fox taught one subject very strongly, for which he faced much opposition even from some of the godliest Puritans of the day, and that is: the purity and holiness of the Christian life. In that day there were Puritans who were formed to face the dead orthodoxy of the time and encourage their churches to holiness of heart and life. Yet though there was much teaching on holiness, there was little appropriation of these truths by the followers of the Puritans; hence they opposed movements like the Quakers who walked in the truths they taught. Hear the lament of Fox over this opposition to the truth:

> But they could not endure to hear of purity, and of victory over sin and the devil. They said they could not believe any could be free from sin on this side of the grave. I bade them give over babbling about the Scriptures, which were holy men's words, whilst they pleaded for unholiness. Then I bade them forbear talking of the Scriptures, which were the holy men's words; "for," said I, "the holy men that wrote the Scriptures pleaded for holiness in heart, life, and conversation here; but since you plead for impurity and sin, which is of the devil, what have you to do with the holy men's words?"[1]

---

1. William Woods Smyth, *Life and Holiness—Substance of Addresses* (London: Elliot Stock, 1884), 40.

He had such boldness before men because he had a familiarity with God. He feared God more than men, and was partial to no man.

My brothers and sisters, believers in our glorious Lord Jesus Christ must not show favoritism (James 2:1).

Therefore, he could say: "When the Lord sent me forth into the world, he forbade me to put off my hat to any, high or low."[2] To live for the glory of God was his supreme desire over worldly vanity and success. The Lord spoke directly and clearly to his heart and he walked in that revelation. "The Lord showed me, so that I did see clearly, that he did not dwell in these temples which men had commanded and set up, but in people's hearts... his people were his temple, and he dwelt in them."[3] Oh how we need many like George Fox to rise up and proclaim fearlessly the apostolic truths that have been long lost in evangelical circles.

Thomas Ellwood, a fellow Friend, speaks of George Fox: "This holy man was raised up by God in an extraordinary manner, for an extraordinary work, even to awaken the sleeping world. He was valiant for truth, bold in asserting it, patient in suffering for it, unwearied in laboring in it, steady in his testimony to it; immovable as a rock."[4]

William Penn, one of the early leaders of the Quaker movement, wrote of Fox: "His ministry and writings show they are from one that was not taught of man... Nor were they notional or speculative, but sensible and practical truths, tending to conversion and regeneration and the setting up of the kingdom of God in the hearts of men... He had an extraordinary gift in

2. George Fox, *Journal of George Fox: Being an Historical Account of the Life, Travels and Labour of love in the work of the ministry* (London: W. & F. G. Cash, 1820), 72.

3. William Carl Placher, *Callings: Twenty Centuries of Christian Wisdom on Vocation*, (Grand Rapids: Eerdmans Publishing, 2005), 295.

4. George Fox, *Journal of George Fox*, Volume 2, (London: Friends Tract Association, 1891), 526.

opening the Scriptures. He would go to the marrow of things… But above all he excelled in prayer."[1]

The impact of his life can hardly be measured. His name carries along with it the life that was burnt out for God. His tombstone reads simply:

Here lies George Fox[2]

---

1. William Penn, *The Select Works of William Penn*, Volume 3, (London, William Phillips, 1825), 452.

2. The original marker has been replaced owing to wear and tear.

CHAPTER 8

Lessons Learned from the Life of George Fox

George Fox is remembered mostly in our day through the legacy of the Quaker movement, which, sadly in the modern day has fallen into great apostasy. Homosexuality, feminism, and all other sorts of straying from the true faith have occurred. Yet during Fox's lifetime and beyond, the Quaker movement was a powerful resurgence of the true apostolic faith in England, and even worldwide. It was a needful time for such a work of God's Spirit in the churches, which in those days fell into dead formalism, commercialism, and state-run entities.

Lesson 1: Different Gifts in the Body of Christ

In the life of George Fox we first see that he was called apart by God for a special purpose in his day. He had a prophetic role in his preaching and life, which set him apart from all other preachers in his day. As John Knox seemed more of a prophet than preacher in Scotland, so George Fox walked about as one of the Old Testament prophets. No man can put a prophetic calling on his life—it can only be received from God. Sadly, self-assumed prophets abound in Christianity in our day, and their lives show forth their spurious calling and pride.

Though George Fox's prophetic calling was overwhelming to many and seemed strongly opposed to traditional practices in his day, still the role of the prophet was fulfilled:

But the one who prophesies speaks to people for their strengthening, encouraging and comfort (1 Cor. 14:3).

So Christ himself gave the apostles, the prophets, the evangelists, the pastors and teachers, to equip his people for works of service, so that the body of Christ may be built up, until we all reach unity in the faith and in the knowledge of the Son of God and become mature, attaining to the whole measure of the fullness of Christ (Eph. 4:11–13).

His ministry raised up many in the body of Christ to fulfill their purpose and callings in God. He did not desire men to follow him only, but he was able to raise up many more in the body of Christ by God's grace. Though some Quakers spoke like George Fox in a prophetic tone, many did not. God was raising up a body of Christ that was balanced with many different gifts and callings in operation. There was a maturity in many believers that was a threat to the established pastors in that day, who capitalized on the religious ignorance of the Scriptures by the masses. The Quaker movement, led by the Spirit of Christ, educated believers into basic principles of the church; and many were used of God to preach the gospel in countries all over the world.

We can learn a lesson that there are different gifts in the body of Christ, and each gift is for the betterment of the entire church. When someone is very different from ourselves in the way they come across, we must have grace and discernment to consider what their calling is from God.

Lesson 2: Preaching Against the Love of Money

One of the qualifications written in the New Testament epistles is that spiritual elders are not to be lovers of money. This theme is clearly carried from the teachings of our Lord, that we cannot serve money as a god and still consider ourselves in the service of the one true God:

No one can serve two masters. Either you will hate the one and love the other, or you will be devoted to the one and despise the other. You cannot serve both God and money (Matt. 6:24).

Not given to drunkenness, not violent but gentle, not quarrelsome, not a lover of money (1 Tim. 3:3).

Fox labored to restore the emphasis of this teaching to England in his day, when abuses of the saddest kind were carried on by clergy and priests. Fox laments: "Oh! The vast sums of money that are gotten by the trade they make of selling the Scriptures, and by their preaching, from the highest bishop to the lowest priest!" Is it no different in our time with modern TV preachers who sell God at a bargain price, sell blessings and prayers, and sell religious trinkets. How we need another prophetic George Fox in our day to speak to this excess by the Spirit of the Lord.

He never spoke on his own authority but relied on the burden of the Lord. We can in our day learn from this burden and ask ourselves the question: Do I love money? Is the love of money contending with my love for God and his ways? Jesus Christ our Lord said we could not love both. The Scriptures are full of commands towards not being greedy or setting ourselves towards monetary gain. As believers in Christ we must be rich towards God and rich in good works. Be open to the Holy Spirit's correction in your life and make changes. God will honor you.

Lesson 3: The Spirit has Come to Teach His People Himself

One of the main burdens of the ministry of George Fox was to release the people of God, who were in great bondage to the religious traditions of England. One chief bondage in the church in his day, which was similar to the Catholic system, was that believers could not teach themselves without a priest. Such superstition and false reliance on human priests abounded in England. At one time it was illegal even to meet as Christians, to baptize, or have communion, without a priest present. The Lord clearly, through the life of George Fox, ministered the truth that God himself has come to teach his people.

> *But when he, the Spirit of truth, comes, he will guide you into all the truth. He will not speak on his own; he will speak only what he hears, and he will tell you what is yet to come* (John 16:13).

As for you, the anointing you received from him remains in you, and you do not need anyone to teach you. But as his anointing teaches you about all things and as that anointing is real, not counterfeit—just as it has taught you, remain in him (1 John 2:27).

The Holy Spirit himself was able to teach the body of Christ and lead people into truth, and they did not have to rely on Church of England clergy. Such thinking in his day was scandalous, and perhaps in our day the same thinking can be scandalous also. Especially in North America, the idea of one pastor as leader of a church has been popularized in evangelicalism. This goes against the clear teachings of Scripture, that God desires many to be raised up to maturity in the body of Christ, and not just one pastor to teach all the flock of God. Fox spoke directly to this abuse so that the entire body of Christ could be released to function in their gifts. This did not negate spiritual leadership, for the Quaker movement, though lay-led, was led also by many with shepherd gifts in the body, such as George Fox and William Penn.

We can learn that the Holy Spirit himself has come to teach us. This does not negate the need to learn from others in the body of Christ, including pastors and teachers. But we must never fully rely on any pastor, no matter how gifted they are. Jesus Christ by his Spirit can be our wonderful teacher as he illuminates the Word of God in our hearts. May God allow a freedom to happen in the body of Christ in our day, so believers can be liberated to be taught by the Holy Spirit.

Lesson 4: Holiness in the Christian Life

Perhaps one of the greatest needs in the church of America today is holiness! When we think of holiness we are not thinking of many small legalistic rules to keep and what not to do. Rather we are speaking of the general tenor of the Christian life. Are we holy towards the Lord for a special purpose? What makes you different from the world around you? There is a popular form of Christianity in our day which looks and acts just like the world.

Such was foreign to the New Testament as well as the Quakers in the day of George Fox.

> *Depart, depart, go out from there! Touch no unclean thing! Come out from it and be pure, you who carry the articles of the Lord's house* (Isa. 52:11).

> *But just as he who called you is holy, so be holy in all you do; for it is written: "Be holy, because I am holy"* (1 Peter 1:15–16).

> *For the grace of God has appeared that offers salvation to all people. It teaches us to say "No" to ungodliness and worldly passions, and to live self-controlled, upright and godly lives in this present age* (Titus 2:11–12).

God calls us to be different from the world around us. Exact rules on what to do in every situation are not given to us in the Scriptures; but general, strong commands to be separate are. Early in the life of George Fox, at nineteen years of age, under family pressure, he was seeking to become a priest through study. It was an experience with corrupt priests who got drunk that set him on a journey to seek God alone to teach him. The unholiness of these professors of faith grieved his heart. May it grieve our hearts also.

> When I came towards nineteen years of age, being upon business at a fair, one of my cousins, whose name was Bradford, having another professor with him, came and asked me to drink part of a jug of beer with them. I, being thirsty, went in with them, for I loved any who had a sense of good, or that sought after the Lord. When we had drunk a glass apiece, they began to drink healths, and called for more drink, agreeing together that he that would not drink should pay all. I was grieved that any who made profession of religion should offer to do so. They grieved me very much, having never had such a thing put to me before by any sort of people. Wherefore I rose up, and, putting my hand in my pocket, took out a groat, and laid it upon the table before them, saying, "If it be so, I will leave you." So I went away; and when I had done my business, returned home; but did not go to bed that night, nor could I sleep, but sometimes walked up and down, and sometimes prayed and cried to the Lord,

who said unto me: "Thou seest how young people go together into vanity, and old people into the earth; thou must forsake all, young and old, keep out of all, and be as a stranger unto all."[1]

Not just priests but all Christians are called to be different to the world around them. May we not follow popular Christianity in our day, but follow the Lord in his ways.

---

1. George Fox, *George Fox - An Autobiography* Chapter 1. Boyhood—A Seeker, accessed June 28, 2014, http://www.strecorsoc.org/gfox/ch01.html.

CHAPTER 9

Inspiring Quotes from George Fox

George Fox, though almost illiterate, became powerful through the pen, and was prolific in writing to many of the leading Christians of the day. One example of this is that he replied personally to every single Puritan tract that was written against the Society of Friends (Quakers). And if that was not enough, he also wrote a challenging tract to John Owen himself who was esteemed head of all the Puritans in that day. What is radical about this is that the Puritans were the "better" Christians in their day amongst a very corrupt Church of England.

Amongst other writings George Fox wrote many epistles to all the scattered meetings of believers, where he exhorted them from the Scriptures. Most of Fox's writings are quotes from various passages of the Bible melded together. He memorized virtually the entirety of the Word of God, so it flew out of him as he wrote. It is highly recommended to our readers who are not acquainted with his writings to find and read a copy of his journals: *The Journals of George Fox.*

Justice Bennet of Derby was the first that called us Quakers, because I bid them tremble at the word of the Lord. This was in the year 1650.

Why should any man have power over any other man's faith, seeing Christ himself is the author of it?

I saw also that there was an ocean of darkness and death, but an infinite ocean of light and love, which flowed over the ocean of darkness.

I knew Jesus, and he was very precious to my soul; but I found something in me that would not keep sweet and patient and kind. I did what I could to keep it down, but it was there. I besought Jesus to do something for me; and when I gave him my will, he came to my heart and took out all that would not be sweet, all that would not be kind, all that would not be patient, and then he shut the door.

Keep within. And when they say, "lo here," or "lo there" is Christ, go not forth; for Christ is within you. And they are seducers and Antichrists which draw your minds out from the teachings within you.

It is said by the professors: "There is no order among you," but I say the order of God is a mystery. Its order will stand when all of theirs is gone. The cry is: "There is no government amongst you!" Is there not? Yes, the government of Christ.

This is the word of the Lord God to you all, a charge to you all in the presence of the living God: be patterns, be examples, in all countries, places, islands, nations, wherever you come; that your carriage and life may preach among all sorts of people, and to them; then you will come to walk cheerfully over the world, answering that of God in every one; whereby in them ye may be a blessing, and make the witness of God in them to bless you: then to the Lord God you will be a sweet savor, and a blessing.

The Lord showed me, so that I did see clearly, that he did not dwell in these temples which men had commanded and set up, but in people's hearts. His people were his temple, and he dwelt in them.

This is the word of the Lord God to you all. The call is now out of transgression, the Spirit bids, come. The call is now from all false worship and gods, from all inventions and dead works, to serve the living God. The call is to repentance, to amendment of life, whereby righteousness may be brought forth, which shall go throughout the earth.

I saw that Christ died for all men, and was a propitiation for all, and enlightened all men and women with his divine and saving light; and that none could be a true believer but who believed in it. I saw that the grace of God, which bringeth salvation, had appeared to all men, and that the manifestation of the Spirit of God was given to every man to profit withal. These things I did not see by the help of man, nor by the letter, though they are written in the letter, but I saw them in the light of the Lord Jesus Christ, and by his immediate spirit and power.

One man raised by God's power to stand and live in the same spirit the apostle and prophets were in, can shake the country for ten miles around.

Therefore this is the word of the Lord to you all, "keep in the wisdom of God" that spreads over all the earth—the wisdom of the creation, that is pure from above, not destructive. For now shall salvation go out of Zion, to judge the mount of Esau. Now shall the law go forth from Jerusalem, to answer the principle of God in all, to hew down all inventors and inventions. For all the princes of the earth are but as air to the power of the Lord God, which you are in, and have tasted of; therefore live in it, that is the word of the Lord God to you all; do not abuse it; keep down and low; and take heed of false joys, that will change.

I asked him [one called Dr. Cradock] why he persecuted Friends for not paying tithes. And whether God ever gave a command to the Gentiles that they should pay tithes. And whether Christ had not ended tithes when he ended the Levitical priesthood that took tithes. And whether Christ, when he sent forth his disciples to preach, had not commanded them to preach freely, as he had given them freely. And whether all ministers of Christ are not bound to observe this command of Christ.

I told them the gospel was the power of God, which was preached before Matthew, Mark, Luke and John or any of them were printed or written; and it was preached to every creature (of which a great part might never see or hear of those four books), so that every creature was to obey the power of God; for Christ, the spiritual Man, would judge the world according to the gospel, that is, according to his invisible power. When they heard this, they could not gainsay, for the truth came over them. I directed them to their teacher, the grace of God, and showed them the sufficiency of it, which would teach them how to live, and what to deny; and being obeyed, would bring them salvation. So to that grace I recommended them, and left them.

You will say, Christ saith this, and the apostles say this; but what canst thou say? Art thou a child of light and hast walked in the light, and what thou speakest, is it inwardly from God?

Therefore be still awhile from thy own thoughts, searching, seeking, desires, and imaginations, and be staid in the principle of God in thee, that it may raise thy mind up to God, and stay it upon God, and thou wilt find strength from him, and find him to be a God at hand, a present help in time of trouble and of need. And thou being come to the principle of God, which hath been transgressed, it will keep thee humble; and the humble, God will teach his way, which is peace, and such he doth exalt.

Therefore ye that be chosen and faithful, who are with the Lamb, go through your work faithfully in the strength and power of the Lord.

Henry Alline

CHAPTER 10

Pen Sketch of Henry Alline

Henry Alline is virtually unknown to modern day Christians, but is well known in heaven. His life was fully spent for God on this earth as he laid up treasures in heaven. The life of Henry Alline is a contradiction to the compromising, convoluted, comfortable Christianity we see today. Alline lost all for God and cared little for the opinions of men. His short life of ministry did more for the cause of the gospel than hundreds of ministers in his day. His life was consumed with eternity. Alline cared not for this life and spent his health, money, time, and energy to serve God acceptably. On horseback he preached the gospel of Jesus Christ to an entire province of souls in less than ten years. Known as the *George Whitefield of Nova Scotia*, he was the instrument God used to send a Great Awakening to this part of Canada.

A Flame of Fire

Professor Benjamin Rand says: "Like a flame of fire he swept through the land at a period when there brooded over Nova Scotia a spirit of darkness."[1] During the times of the Great Awakening in America, God raised up a man who had his view set firmly on eternity. Alline did not just preach a gospel but rather an everlasting gospel in which he pleaded for men to justly

---

1. Benjamin Rand was born in Canning, Nova Scotia, in 1856. He graduated from Acadia University with a B.A. in 1875 and an M.A. in 1879 and from Harvard University with a Ph.D. in 1885. He subsequently embarked on a career at Harvard that included stints as Assistant in Philosophy from 1892–1897, Instructor from 1897–1902, and finally Philosophical Librarian from 1906 until his retirement in 1933.

believe. Alline was a man who burned out for God, laboring until he could labor no more. Oh, how we need to see men again in our generation full of energy and usefulness to God. Alline fully committed all of himself to the work of God, leaving nothing for himself. His conversion in Nova Scotia, Canada, marked a time that the land would never forget. As his entire ministry, his conversion experience was drastic and bold. Years of time passed before he came to a full assurance of calling into the ministry and peace with God. His calling into ministry and shouts of victory echoed into the darkness as demons shuddered at the full resignation of a will to God:

> My soul was set at liberty, the Lord discovered to me my labor in the ministry and call to preach the gospel. I cried out "Amen, I'll go, I'll go, send me, send me." His cry was continually: "O eternity, eternity, unfathomable eternity! The joy of the righteous but the dread of the wicked."[1]

Such a mindset and ministry was effective in bringing multitudes into the kingdom of God. One stanza of a hymn, one of five hundred hymns Alline published in his lifetime, reflects this truth:

> O what a day! how ill the wicked stand. What scenes immortal open to their view? All time deserted, mortal changes past. And they awake, before the awful Bar, where grace and hope to them are known no more.[2]

Souls Kept Blind

A frowning world is what any true gospel preacher approaches—a world that crucified Christ and hates God. The Scriptures share this sobering reality: "Marvel not, my brethren, if the world hate you." Henry Alline experienced this hatred from the lost

1. Henry Alline, *The Life and Journal of the Rev. Mr. Henry Alline* (Gilbert & Dean, 1806).

2. George A. Rawlyk, *Henry Alline: Selected Writings* (Mahwah: Paulist Press, 1987), 74.

souls that he pleaded with and even more from the established religious elite. Yet amidst such opposition, Alline could joyfully write in his journal: "Although there was much opposition from earth and hell, the work of God was still reviving." And again: "I preached very often, and the people seemed to be alarmed and greatly attentive to the gospel. I returned through Horton again, where I met with some opposition. But God was kind to me, and gave me strength to face a frowning world."[3]

Without being frightened in any way by those who oppose you. This is a sign to them that they will be destroyed, but that you will be saved—and that by God. For it has been granted to you on behalf of Christ not only to believe in him, but also to suffer for him (Phil. 1:28–29).

Alline preached an uncompromising standard and a biblical gospel that made many in his day raise their arms in protest. He found a principle very quickly in his ministry, and stated it repeatedly in his journals:

O the damage that is done by unconverted ministers and legal professors. I have found them in my travels more inveterate against the power of religion than the openly profane. These unconverted ministers, false professors, unregenerate priests stood firmly against the preaching of repentance, holiness, and a conversion experience.

To suggest that any of these ministers' congregants were unregenerate would put their preaching in question, therefore they labored to silence Alline many times. He writes:

Thousands of souls are kept blind, until they are gone beyond all recovery. To carry on this infernal scheme, a number of anti-Christian ministers are laboring night and day to prove that a feeling knowledge of redemption in the soul is not to be attained and that all such pretensions are a vain imagination and a delusion; and tell their hearers, if they do so and so, and are baptized, join the church, come to the Lord's table, and do their best in those outward things, all will be well. And thus they are murdering the precious and

---

3. Henry Alline, *The Life and Journal of the Rev. Mr. Henry Alline* (Gilbert & Dean, 1806).

immortal souls about them. O that God would awaken and convert them, or remove them. And O that all mankind would believe that they need to be redeemed.[1]

Alline agreed with the views of Gilbert Tennent towards unconverted ministers and their lack of ability to convert souls to God. Here is an excerpt of a sermon by Tennant which Alline could have read in his day:

> I am verily persuaded the generality of preachers talk of an unknown and unfelt Christ; and the reason why congregations have been so dead is because they have dead men preaching to them. O that the Lord may quicken and revive them for his own name's sake. For how can dead men beget living children?[2]

Bodily Infirmities

Henry Alline was well acquainted with suffering. His life followed the path of many of God's generals: Brainerd, Hyde, McCheyne, and others. His life bore witness to the unchanging truth of Scripture: "He chose to be mistreated along with the people of God rather than to enjoy the fleeting pleasures of sin" (Heb. 11:25). The list of the faithful in Hebrews 11 parallels Alline's life when it says:

> *Some faced jeers and flogging, and even chains and imprisonment. They were put to death by stoning; they were sawed in two; they were killed by the sword. They went about in sheepskins and goatskins, destitute, persecuted and mistreated—the world was not worthy of them. They wandered in deserts and mountains, living in caves and in holes in the ground* (Heb. 11:36–38).

Being destitute, afflicted, tormented; bodily afflictions and infirmities were commonplace for Alline. For him to labor for the gospel was much more important than keeping perfect

---

1. Ibid.

2. Maurice Whitman Armstrong, *The Great Awakening in Nova Scotia, 1776–1809* (American Society of Church History, 1948), 6.

health or having no pain. Such thinking today would not only border on legalism in many Christian circles, but fanaticism and even insanity.

Read some accounts from his journals showing the holy recklessness he had as the gospel march drew him onward in complete and utter abandonment to eternity and its values:

> Rode 30 miles this day; and although I was so fatigued by riding in heavy rain that I could scarcely walk when I got from my horse, yet when I began to preach, I had such a sense of the Redeemer's cause, that I almost forgot my bodily infirmities.[3]

> I preached so often and rode so much that sometimes I would seem almost worn out and yet in a few hours would be so refreshed, that I could labor again for twelve hours in discoursing, praying, preaching, and exhorting, and feel strong in my lungs.[4]

> About the first of September I was taken with a very sore throat, occasioned by swelling, which continued some days; so that I could swallow nothing but a few spoonfuls of liquids for my support, but was enabled to speak in public when at the worst, to my own astonishment and the astonishment of the others also.[5]

The acute awareness that he had contracted tuberculosis drove Alline to labor for the gospel even more intently. He relentlessly preached and traveled, crying to a deaf and blind humanity the message of the cross of Christ. He became very ill, and by 1783 he had driven himself to the very end of his endurance. He died in New England after evangelizing the entire province of Nova Scotia in less than ten years! At thirty-five years young, this fervent, pleading, robust man of God breathed his last. Only heaven knows the fruits of his labors. Alline lost his health for God.

---

3. Henry Alline, *The Life and Journal of the Rev. Mr. Henry Alline* (Gilbert & Dean, 1806)

4. Ibid.

5. Ibid.

A Tombstone Cries Out!

W. B. Bezanson gave this testimony: "Henry Alline yielded his life in complete compliance to the plan of God. Oh cannot this be for us? Cannot we surrender all in obedience to the precious gospel of our Savior, the Lord Jesus Christ? If he is not Lord of all, he is not Lord! Present yourselves to God as those who have been brought from death to life, and your members to God as instruments for righteousness."[1]

Alline's last words were: "Now I rejoice in Jesus."[2] After a short life of ministry with God he gave up the ghost. Do you think he is going to stand before the judgment bar of God, ashamed at a life that was selfish and held onto its own through self-preservation? Perhaps Alline's response to such a thought as this would be: Away with self! Crucify it! Put it to death. Oh the miserable thing of self! All to Christ, all to God, does he deserve anything less?

For whoever wants to save their life will lose it, but whoever loses their life for me will save it. What good is it for someone to gain the whole world, and yet lose or forfeit their very self? (Luke 9:24–25).

Whoever does not take up their cross and follow me is not worthy of me (Matt. 10:38).

After all the trials and tribulations he endured for the sake of the gospel, Alline has entered his rest. Yet alas, Christians in our day are resting and taking it easy as a damned world slips into a hell without exits. Alline saw this reality, and with the saintly Andrew Bonar cried in his spirit: "Oh they perish! they perish!"[3] The Puritans were known to say that we must go through hell to get to heaven. And how true that statement is. Dear believer,

---

1. W. B. Bezanson, *Romance of Religion: A Sketch of the Life of Henry Alline in the Pioneer Days of the Maritime Provinces* (Kentville, Kentville Publishing, 1927).

2. Henry Alline, *The Life and Journal of the Rev. Mr. Henry Alline* (Gilbert & Dean, 1806).

3. Leonard Ravenhill, *Why Revival Tarries* (Bloomington, Bethany House Publishers, 1987), 43.

this is our hell—this earth. The wiles of sin and the temptations of the devil are the believer's hell. The worst the Christian will experience in this life is the myriad temptations of the flesh, the world, and the devil; and then we will enter into all the joys of heaven and God.

> *In this world you will have trouble. But take heart! I have overcome the world* (John 16:33в).

> *For our light and momentary troubles are achieving for us an eternal glory that far outweighs them all* (2 Cor. 4:17).

Yet for the masses of mankind it is not so! May God sober us to realize not only our portion but the portion of the wicked also, as it says in the Proverbs:

> *When calamity comes, the wicked are brought down, but even in death the righteous seek refuge in God* (Prov. 14:32).

Henry Alline died at the age of 35. Like a flame of fire he had swept through the land in his zealous travels in the cause of Christ. Languishing on the way, he cheerfully resigned his life. His tombstone reads: "Rev. Henry Alline 1748-1784. He was a burning and shining light and was justly esteemed the Apostle of Nova Scotia." His gravestone sits before us as a landmark of what a life can do for God in this earthly sojourn. It speaks loudly against our laxity, superficiality, liberalism, and mediocrity in the things of God. It cries out to a lost mankind that is going to an eternal hell with everlasting burnings and torment.

> *Then death and Hades were thrown into the lake of fire. The lake of fire is the second death. Anyone whose name was not found written in the book of life was thrown into the lake of fire* (Rev. 20:14–15).

It laments over our lack of vigor to live and die for the Savior of our souls, giving lip service to the King and living as if there were no cross. Shall we stand before his tombstone and with tears in our eyes say "God make me such a flame for thee"? Oh may God raise up more of these flames of fire in our generation to sweep across the land of Canada in revival fire. May it be so, Amen.

CHAPTER 11

Lessons Learned from the Life of Henry Alline

Convicting, challenging, stirring—these are just some of the adjectives that come to mind when one gives a brief look at the life of Alline. Sadly, many contemporary scholars and theologians in the Nova Scotia area have alluded to the probability of Alline's mental derangement from being exposed to thoughts of hell too early in his life. Oh how utterly foolish the modern mind is in light of the truth of eternity and an eternal God. Alline knew more of God than most, if not all, modern preachers in Canada, and had a depth of awe and fear of his ways and judgment. We have much to learn from this apostle of the faith and also much to apply in our modern lives. May we humbly try to learn some lessons from this precious saint's life.

Lesson 1: Burning out for God

This concept of expending energy for God to the place where one physically wears himself out is considered a foolish thing to modern believers. The same recklessness seen in pioneer missions to foreign countries also seems like a waste to the modern American mind. How could it be profitable for a missionary family to go to Africa when they will lose their children there within a few years and even themselves die? Yet this was the way for many of God's chosen saints who suffered at great lengths to spread the gospel of Jesus Christ to the world. So what is the logic that they had, which gave them the desire to go and expend their physical lives prematurely for Christ? The answer is simply that they saw the great value of Jesus Christ and eternity, and the worth of expending all one's life energies here in his service. These saints of old knew that life was short and passing, and they heeded the admonition of their Lord to store up treasures in heaven not in the earth. The concept of rewards in heaven is something evangelicals in our day know little or nothing about. The biblical fact is that the Lord will reward believers in eternity; this does not negate free grace in the blood of Christ. The importance of rewards in heaven is a large theme in the New Testament writings.

Here are some verses that will help you start to consider why Henry Alline willingly pushed himself to the place of exhaustion and death for the sake of Christ:

> *Whatever you do, work at it with all your heart, as working for the Lord, not for human masters, since you know that you will receive an inheritance from the Lord as a reward. It is the Lord Christ you are serving* (Col. 3:23–24).

> *Command them to do good, to be rich in good deeds, and to be generous and willing to share. In this way they will lay up treasure for themselves as a firm foundation for the coming age, so that they may take hold of the life that is truly life* (1 Tim. 6:18–19).

> *Watch out that you do not lose what we have worked for, but that you may be rewarded fully* (2 John 1:8).

> *Look, I am coming soon! My reward is with me, and I will give to each person according to what they have done* (Rev. 22:12).

Alline knew that he could not do anything to make himself more saved, for the righteousness of Christ was sufficient. But he did see that what he did on the earth now would matter greatly in heaven. What he sowed now he would reap later. He saw the great burden of his God for lost men and women and shared that passion. He willingly suffered now so he could be crowned later. Many of God's choice servants suffered greatly in this life and even had early deaths. Was it a waste? No! Ten thousand times, No! They saw the reward. They saw the eternal weight of glory.

What of you, my friend? Are you going to play it safe your entire life? Seek comfort as a god? Or will you choose to suffer in some way, bear some inconveniences for the sake of the spread of the gospel in this generation?

Lesson 2: Having A Zeal for Spreading the Gospel

Henry Alline was no one special. He was a blood-bought servant of Jesus Christ who felt the great burden of his Lord for a lost and dying humanity. He labored where he saw the need, and it was all around him. Nova Scotia, Canada, became his mission field; the horse his means; and the gospel his message. He set out to evangelize every single individual in Nova Scotia, and that he did! He established over a hundred congregations and on horseback traveled to every single town and village to share the good news of Jesus Christ, the Savior from sin.

We can learn this wonderful lesson from Alline: that no cost is too great to share the gospel message with others. How can we who have received such a wondrous message of salvation keep it to ourselves? How can we who share in the very life of Jesus Christ and his peace not tell others of it who have no peace and are tormented in their dark hearts? Though we might not be called to evangelize every person in our state, each of us are called to be lights in the world for our Lord to others:

You are the light of the world. A town built on a hill cannot be hidden (Matt. 5:14).

Then he said to his disciples, "The harvest is plentiful but the workers are few. Ask the Lord of the harvest, therefore, to send out workers into his harvest field" (Matt. 9:37–38).

Christian life can be confused with so many different ideas and concepts. But the one clear truth in the Word of God is that we are saved by the gospel of Jesus Christ and then must share this gospel with others. Our Lord himself gave every single disciple the command to share the gospel with the world:

He said to them, "Go into all the world and preach the gospel to all creation" (Mark 16:15).

Therefore go and make disciples of all nations, baptizing them in the name of the Father and of the Son and of the Holy Spirit, and teaching them to obey everything I have commanded you. And surely I am with you always, to the very end of the age (Matt. 28:19–20).

But you will receive power when the Holy Spirit comes on you; and you will be my witnesses in Jerusalem, and in all Judea and Samaria, and to the ends of the earth (Acts 1:8).

Alline heard the call from his master and was not disobedient. Will you hear the call and start to share the gospel in any way you can with others?

Lesson 3: An Eternal Hell is Real

Henry Alline believed in an eternal hell where those who did not have their sins washed by the blood of the Lamb would spend eternity in the wrath of the Lamb. He saw that God himself will judge and throw those who do not obey the gospel of Jesus Christ into an eternal punishment. Oh, how serious it was to him as he preached before men and women, children and elderly. He saw their estate as apart from God and needing to be reconciled and born-again by the Spirit of God. He called for repentance and belief in the good news of Jesus Christ. Alline cries out: "O that all mankind would believe that they need to be redeemed."

The belief in hell or its eternity is being questioned by modern minds. They are saying this is a cruel, archaic belief that made people scared of God and therefore subservient to the Roman Church. Though the message of hell was used by Catholics to at times scare common folk into their sacraments, this by no means negates its truth. Jesus Christ taught clearly on the truth that there is an eternal hell and made it very clear that it would be better for one to even lose limbs in this life, and then go to heaven, rather than to go to hell:

If your right eye causes you to stumble, gouge it out and throw it away. It is better for you to lose one part of your body than for your whole body to be thrown into hell (Matt 5:29).

Do not be afraid of those who kill the body but cannot kill the soul. Rather, be afraid of the one who can destroy both soul and body in hell (Matt. 10:28).

Then he will say to those on his left, "Depart from me, you who are cursed, into the eternal fire prepared for the devil and his angels" (Matt. 25:41).

But the cowardly, the unbelieving, the vile, the murderers, the sexually immoral, those who practice magic arts, the idolaters and all liars—they will be consigned to the fiery lake of burning sulfur. This is the second death (Rev. 21:8).

The modern gospel says that hell is not really that bad or perhaps even non-existent. But the true gospel says to flee from the wrath to come! Oh how we need to recapture the truth of an eternal hell; would that not change everything? Now you understand why Alline spent himself so readily in the service of his Lord. He saw the cliff of eternity and the masses rushing on without knowledge of what was ahead. Modern mankind is in a busy frenzy of doing everything but considering this truth. Hell is greedily yawning its mouth. May we see its horror and the enormity of our sins before a holy God. Turn and repent and look to the precious Son of God, Jesus Christ, to be saved. Time is fleeing.

CHAPTER 12

Inspiring Quotes from Henry Alline

Little if anything is known of Henry Alline in Canada, or the world, by most Christians today. I personally took a visit to Acadia Divinity School in Nova Scotia to read his journals and writings, which are archived there. One of the great blessings for me in this trip was to be able to see his old gravestone which is in the lower level of the seminary. It was a moving experience to be able to say a prayer and have a time of reflection upon this dear brother's life that was so consecrated to the Lord's work. Though there are not many quotes included here, it will give a sense of the enormity of this man's vision of God and also of sin, hell, and eternity!

Redeeming love broke into my soul… with such power that my whole soul seemed to be melted down with love… and my will turned of choice after the infinite God.

I had this day a great sense of the emptiness and vanity of all things here below. If I had millions and millions of worlds, they would not make me happy. Christ is all in all; in him I find a solid peace.

I thought very much of the goodness of God to me in giving me one more moment for repentance, and that there appeared yet a possibility of my being saved.

God stoops to converse with the inhabitants of time.

Why, why O ye sons and daughters of Adam, will you perish with life eternal at your door? Why will ye despair when Jesus pleads? Why will ye sink when Jesus rises? Why will you die when Jesus lives? Why will you wander in the dark surrounded with the sun in its meridian brightness? Why will you famish with thirst so near the wells of salvation and rivers of eternal pleasure? Why will you starve in a land of plenty, and rush to hell so nigh the gates of heaven?

> Fly wretched mortal from the gulf of hell,
> Forever in the heart of glory dwell,
> and share in joys beyond what tongue can tell!

Adieu to earth

> Adieu to earth with all your joy,
> Adieu to all below;
> Your pleasures all I'd count away,
> If I must Jesus know.

Death reign'd

> Death reign'd with vigor since the fall,
> And rides with fury still;
> Nor rich nor poor, nor great nor small,
> Can e'er resist his will.

And did'st thou die for me

> And did'st thou die for me
> O thou blest Lamb of God?
> And hast thou brought me home to thee;
> By thy own precious blood?

Let angels boast

> Let angels boast their joys above,
> I taste the same below,
> They drink of the Redeemer's love,
> And I have Jesus too.

O that I could a moment expel the interposing cloud that holds you ignorant of thy Creator's love, and point you to the bleeding wounds of that compassionate Savior that now stands at thy door! Ah, how would you in a moment bid adieu to all other lovers, tread every power of your ravished soul.

O what a day! How will the wicked stand, When scenes immortal open to their view? All time deserted, mortal changes past, And they awake before the awful Bar, Where grace and hope to them are known no more.

O for the meekness of the Lamb, to walk with thee, my God! Then should I feel thy lovely name, And feed upon thy Word.

Afterword

CHAPTER 13

Answering the Call in Our Generation

The Psalmist penned this startling observation in his day but how true it is for us as it speaks of our current situation today:

Help, Lord, for no one is faithful anymore; those who are loyal have vanished from the human race (Psa. 12:1).

C.H. Surgeon states of this verse:

For the godly man ceaseth; the death, departure, or decline of godly men should be a trumpet call for more prayer.

As we read old books of saints from past centuries we realize quickly that there is a lack of quality in leadership in the church, especially in the West. Where are the men of God in our day that truly know God deeply, who are apostles, and even prophets—those who walk after God in the power of his might?

In the first epistle of the apostle Peter we are called to be strangers in this world, a people set apart to God and his purposes. Those who are godly men became this by God's grace and followed Christ in the narrow way. It is the way of caring more about the opinion of God than the opinions of men, and more importantly, serving Christ for his glory and name, not for personal ambitions or denominational pursuits. Men such as Moody, Finney, Wesley, Whitefield, Payson, Bounds, Ravenhill, and many others come to mind. They were men who were heavenly-minded and sought God for God himself.

To be men of another sort—a different race of men—is the calling of Christ for us. As we become children of God we become a holy nation set apart for the purposes of our King in heaven.

But you are a chosen people, a royal priesthood, a holy nation, God's special possession, that you may declare the praises of him who called you out of darkness into his wonderful light (1 Peter 2:9).

In other passages in the New Testament we are described as distinctly set apart as a new race of men. God categorizes the world into three races: Jews, Gentiles and the church. And our race is called to be set apart from the customs, practices, and lifestyles of the others. Is your goal godliness? Is your desire to be conformed to the image of Christ and follow him no matter what the cost? The reason there are so few in our day that love the Lord fully, and are whole-hearted, is because so few are willing to walk alone.

For everyone looks out for their own interests, not those of Jesus Christ. But you know that Timothy has proved himself, because as a son with his father he has served with me in the work of the gospel (Phil 2:21–22).

The call to be set apart means exactly that! To be set apart. Any man of God that has been used for the purposes of building the kingdom of God has suffered, walked in lonely paths, and trusted in God and not in themselves.

Now faith is confidence in what we hope for and assurance about what we do not see. This is what the ancients were commended for (Heb. 11:1–2).

He chose to be mistreated along with the people of God rather than to enjoy the fleeting pleasures of sin. He regarded disgrace for the sake of Christ as of greater value than the treasures of Egypt, because he was looking ahead to his reward (Heb. 11:25–26).

It has been the same since the beginning and will be until the end: only the narrow way of following the Lord will produce the godly men he desires. I would also comment that most, if not all, the men whom God ended up using powerfully—men we recognize and quote—were men who did not seek fame but Christ alone. Most, if not all, of these men desired nothing—no ministry, no book, no title, no church; they wanted desperately to obey their Lord in simple obedience out of love for him who paid so much for their salvation by his blood.

So yes, the godly are no more. There is a lack of those who are fully committed to our Lord Jesus Christ in our day. There have been many who have compromised, who have fallen into sin and have shamed the name. But God still desires to see those who will accomplish his purpose in our day. The call is going out; will you hear this call?

> *Since God had planned something better for us so that only together with us would they be made perfect* (Heb. 11:40).

> *For, "Everyone who calls on the name of the Lord will be saved." How, then, can they call on the one they have not believed in? And how can they believe in the one of whom they have not heard? And how can they hear without someone preaching to them? And how can anyone preach unless they are sent? As it is written: "How beautiful are the feet of those who bring good news!"* (Rom. 10:13–15).

Maybe some of you have failed terribly and feel the Lord could not use you again. But consider the apostle Peter, who even denied his Lord three times and yet Jesus restored him in a powerful way to lead his church. So look to Christ, follow him, learn from the godly men of the past, but do not esteem them too highly. Follow God for the sake of God and he will use you in his timing and his ways.

Prophets Needed Again!

In the days of Amos the prophet, there was a weariness in the people of God. The prophetic preaching that the people used to hear stopped. Where was the mouthpiece for God?

> *"The days are coming," declares the Sovereign Lord, "when I will send a famine through the land—not a famine of food or a thirst for water, but a famine of hearing the words of the Lord. People will stagger from sea to sea and wander from north to east, searching for the word of the Lord, but they will not find it"* (Amos 8:11–12).

In the Old Covenant there was a reliance on the man who was in touch with God. Such a person was the communication between God and men. Moses was a great model of this, where the people were frightened to seek God themselves so they forced Moses to be their representative. Even God said to Moses that he would make him like God to the people, so they would hear his words as the words of God himself. Such was the atmosphere of a constant longing for those that would bring the word of the Lord to the people of Israel. When trouble occurred, or major problems, the first thing in people's hearts was: what is God saying? Where is God's prophet of the hour?

In the New Covenant there are not only prophets that lead the people of God, but also pastors, teachers, evangelists, and apostles. Yet the role of the prophet is still important and vital for the church. Sadly, few in our day esteem or desire this calling to be one who is 100 percent uncompromising to the truths of God's Word. There are self-proclaimed prophets who are seeking the honor of men. Such have never been called of God and are warped and self-deceived. Yet there are those few who have been in the school of God for many years—unknown, hidden, and at God's will they come forth to speak for God boldly without the fear of man. Such true prophets are sorely needed in our day to share the heart of God with us. The gift of teaching is very important for the daily and on-going health of the body of Christ. Yet the role of prophet will fulfill and help in ways teachers would never be able to.

When apostasy and false teaching is abounding, then the prophets are needed to stand against the tide of falsehood with the piercing truth of God. Any saint of God can be called for this role, yet God is very selective in his raising of them. God will bring you to the place of nothing before he raises you up to use you in this capacity. Though God has used Bible colleges and seminaries to raise up godly leaders, those who are called to this prophetic role will usually not be birthed from these institutions. When God needed an apostle without compromise, he had to take him to the desert of Arabia and Damascus for fourteen years to train him in the ways of God. Such a message did not come from men or traditions, but God himself revealed it to Paul by revelation:

I did not receive it from any man, nor was I taught it; rather, I received it by revelation from Jesus Christ (Gal. 1:12).

You could imagine the discussion between people in that day, with some stating which apostle mentored them or what Bible school they went to, and then Paul being asked, and his reply is simple: "Oh yes, well Jesus himself came and revealed the gospel to me." There would have been no higher boast than this, or credentials if one needed them. Though there is much to learn from God, prophets are God-trained by his Spirit, so their reliance is on God, not men.

Today, there is a famine of hearing the true words of the Lord. But there is not a famine in hearing of many false teachers who are coming in the name of God but misleading people. So many are teaching false doctrines for the sake of financial prosperity. Sadly, many are believing these false teachers and allowing themselves to be deceived by these charlatans. The apostle Peter wrote of these men two thousand years ago:

> *In their greed these teachers will exploit you with fabricated stories. Their condemnation has long been hanging over them, and their destruction has not been sleeping* (2 Peter 2:3).

The love of money and greediness is the chief characteristic of a false teacher. So when you hear these men on TV going on and on about money, you can assume they could fall into this category. Sadly, discernment in the body of Christ is very low in our day, and many are not reading their Bibles diligently. If we studied our Bibles daily with great diligence, we would know the truth and not be deceived. Our Lord Jesus said it so clearly:

> *Then you will know the truth, and the truth will set you free* (John 8:32).

And the truth firstly sets you free from being deceived by false teachers and prophets in these last days. God has always been faithful to have a voice in every generation. Surely we find ourselves in such a time as the Psalmist lamented:

> *We are given no signs from God; no prophets are left, and none of us knows how long this will be* (Psa. 74:9).

Yet they will come! The prophets will come with messages that will sear our consciences. Oh how we need a modern day prophet. We can be assured that God will never leave a generation without a witness of his working. Especially in the last days, God will revive his church and build a name for himself in the earth, to send out an end-times final witness of the gospel—one just like Jeremiah, who was a prophet that heard from God, and he prophesied:

> *Therefore this is what the Lord God Almighty says: "Because the people have spoken these words, I will make my words in your mouth a fire and these people the wood it consumes"* (Jer. 5:14).

This new breed of preachers will be men that are shut-in with God and hear from him, and their words will be as *fire* and the people *wood*. We must pray in these last days that God will send and raise up these men to help correct and protect the body of Christ from coming deceptions that will come in the last days. And maybe God is even calling you to be his man for this generation, so spend much time in his presence and fear only God and not men. May the Lord do this all for his glorious bride today. Let it be so!

The Call for Action

Perhaps you have been greatly challenged by these writings. Perhaps they have convicted you. That is a good thing, yet we must go towards action and not be content with being a bit disturbed. You can be used in powerful ways just like these men of old. You will not look like them and definitely not sound like them, but God can use you and make you his instrument in this modern generation.

We have learned much from the lives of Whitefield, Cennick, Fox, and Alline. They have shown us what true *Uncompromising Faith* looks like in different ways. Much still has not been shared of these men but it will suffice to say we have learned something of how God sets apart his servants in every generation.

Continue the journey with the Lord. Let him use you, though it will make you alone and separate from others. Others may be doing many compromising things in this generation, but you cannot! God has his call on your life. He is showing you truth. He is showing you the path that the Lord Jesus Christ walked. Follow him in this way.

We close with the words of the late Leonard Ravenhill. May the Lord answer this prayer speedily in our generation, and not just for the pulpits of the land but for every single believer who loves Jesus Christ, that there would be no compromise or guile found but a sense of the presence of the Lord in each life and a clear vision of eternity:

> God of Whitefield, give us today men like Whitefield who can stand as giants in the pulpit, men with burdened hearts, burning lips, and brimming eyes. And, Lord, please do it soon![1]

---

1. Leonard Ravenhill, "George Whitefield: Portrait of a Revival Preacher," accessed July 1, 2014, http://www.ravenhill.org/whitefield.htm.

Purchase additional copies at our website:
www.KingsleyPress.com

This book is also available as an eBook for
Kindle, iBooks, Nook and Kobo.

Also from Kingsley Press:

AN ORDERED LIFE

AN AUTOBIOGRAPHY BY G. H. LANG

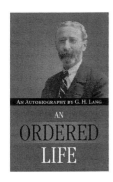

G. H. Lang was a remarkable Bible teacher, preacher and writer of a past generation who should not be forgotten by today's Christians. He inherited the spiritual "mantle" of such giants in the faith as George Müller, Anthony Norris Groves and other notable saints among the early Brethren movement. He traveled all over the world with no fixed means of support other than prayer and faith and no church or other organization to depend on. Like Mr. Müller before him, he told his needs to no one but God. Many times his faith was tried to the limit, as funds for the next part of his journey arrived only at the last minute and from unexpected sources.

This autobiography traces in precise detail the dealings of God with his soul, from the day of his conversion at the tender age of seven, through the twilight years when bodily infirmity restricted most of his former activities. You will be amazed, as you read these pages, to see how quickly and continually a soul can grow in grace and in the knowledge of spiritual things if they will wholly follow the Lord.

Horace Bushnell once wrote that every man's life is a plan of God, and that it's our duty as human beings to find and follow that plan. As Mr. Lang looks back over his long and varied life in the pages of this book, he frequently points out the many times God prepared him in the present for some future work or role. Spiritual life applications abound throughout the book, making it not just a life story but a spiritual training manual of sorts. Preachers will find sermon starters and illustrations in every chapter. Readers of all kinds will benefit from this close-up view of the dealings of God with the soul of one who made it his life's business to follow the Lamb wherever He should lead.

Buy online at our website: **www.KingsleyPress.com**
Also available as an eBook for Kindle, Nook and iBooks.

MEMOIRS OF DAVID STONER

EDITED BY
WILLIAM DAWSON & JOHN HANNAH

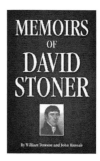

The name of David Stoner (1794-1826) deserves to be ranked alongside those of Robert Murray McCheyne, David Brainerd and Henry Martyn. Like them, he died at a relatively young age; and like them, his life was marked by a profound hunger and thirst for God and intense passion for souls. Stoner was saved at twelve years of age and from that point until his untimely death twenty years later his soul was continually on full stretch for God.

This book tells the story of his short but amazing life: his godly upgringing, his radical conversion, his call to preach, his amazing success as a Wesleyan Methodist preacher, his patience in tribulation and sickness, and his glorious departure to be with Christ forever. Many pages are devoted to extracts from his personal diary which give an amazing glimpse into the heart of one whose desires were all aflame for more of God.

Oswald J. Smith, in his soul-stirring book, *The Revival We Need*, wrote the following: "Have been reading the diary of David Stoner. How I thank God for it! He is another Brainerd. Have been much helped, but how ashamed and humble I feel as I read it! Oh, how he thirsted and searched after God! How he agonized and travailed! And he died at 32."

You, too can be much helped in your spiritual life as you study the life of this youthful saint of a past generation.

"Be instant and constant in prayer. Study, books, eloquence, fine sermons are all nothing without prayer. Prayer brings the Spirit, the life, the power." —*David Stoner*

Buy online at our website: **www.KingsleyPress.com**
Also available as an eBook for Kindle, Nook and iBooks.

ANTHONY NORRIS GROVES
SAINT AND PIONEER
by G. H. Lang

Although his name is little known in Christian circles today, Anthony Norris Groves (1795-1853) was,
according to the writer of this book, one of the most
influential men of the nineteenth century. He was
what might be termed a spiritual pioneer, forging a
path through unfamiliar territory in order that others might follow. One of those who followed him was
George Müller, known to the world as one who in his
lifetime cared for over ten thousand orphans without

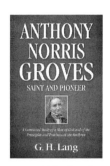

any appeal for human aid, instead trusting God alone to provide for the
daily needs of this large enterprise.

In 1825 Groves wrote a booklet called *Christian Devotedness* in
which he encouraged fellow believers and especially Christian workers
to take literally Jesus' command not to lay up treasures on earth, but
rather to give away their savings and possessions toward the spread of
the gospel and to embark on a life of faith in God alone for the neces-
saries of life. Groves himself took this step of faith: he gave away his for-
tune, left his lucrative dental practice in England, and went to Baghdad
to establish the first Protestant mission to Arabic-speaking Muslims.
His going was not in connection with any church denomination or missionary society, as he sought to rely on God alone for needed finances.
He later went to India also.

His approach to missions was to simplify the task of churches and
missions by returning to the methods of Christ and His apostles, and to
help indigenous converts form their own churches without dependence
on foreign support. His ideas were considered radical at the time but
later became widely accepted in evangelical circles.

Groves was a leading figure in the early days of what Robert Govett
would later call the mightiest movement of the Spirit of God since Pen-
tecost—a movement that became known simply as the Brethren. In this
book G. H. Lang combines a study of the life and influence of Anthony
Norris Groves with a survey of the original principles and practices of
the Brethren movement.

The Christian Hero
A Sketch of the Life of Robert Annan

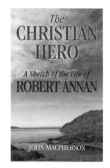

If you've never heard of Robert Annan of Dundee, otherwise known as "the Christian Hero," prepare to be astounded at the amazing grace of God in his life as you turn the pages of this incredible little biography. Its thrilling story will stir you to the depths and almost certainly drive you to your knees with an increased desire to be used for God's glory.

The record of his beginning years reads much like that of John Newton—a life of wandering far from God in the ways of sin and rebellion. At least once he miraculously escaped death through the overruling providence of God. As time passed, he became thoroughly discontented with his sinful life; but he didn't want anything to do with God or Christianity. He thought he could overcome sin and live a morally good life by his own efforts. He soon discovered, however, that he was no match for sin or Satan; and casting himself entirely on God's grace and mercy in Jesus Christ, he was gloriously saved.

From the very first day of his conversion, he became a tireless seeker of lost souls. He worked during the day time as a stone mason, but his evenings and weekends were spent preaching in the streets or in homes. Frequently he would spend whole nights in secret prayer, pleading at the throne of grace for lost sinners. As he went to his employment in the early mornings, he would often write Scripture verses on the pavement for others to read as they passed by on their way to work or school. Thus he was instant in season and out of season, using every opportunity to present to men the claims of Jesus Christ and the reality of heaven, hell, and the judgment that awaits every human soul.

Read his story and be amazed, remembering that what God did for Robert Annan he can and will do for anyone.

GIPSY SMITH
HIS LIFE AND WORK

This autobiography of Gipsy Smith (1860-1947) tells the fascinating story of how God's amazing grace reached down into the life of a poor, uneducated gipsy boy and sent him singing and preaching all over Britain and America until he became a household name in many parts and influenced the lives of millions for Christ. He was born and raised in a gipsy tent to parents who made a living selling baskets, tinware and clothes pegs. His father was in and out of jail for various offences, but was gloriously converted during an evangelistic meeting. His mother died when he was only five years old.

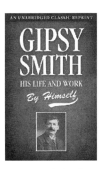

Converted at the age of sixteen, Gipsy taught himself to read and write and began to practice preaching. His beautiful singing voice earned him the nickname "the singing gipsy boy," as he sang hymns to the people he met. At age seventeen he became an evangelist with the Christian Mission (which became the Salvation Army) and began to attract large crowds. Leaving the Salvation Army in 1882, he became an itinerant evangelist working with a variety of organizations. It is said that he never had a meeting without conversions. He was a born orator. One of the Boston papers described him as "the greatest of his kind on earth, a spiritual phenomenon, an intellectual prodigy and a musical and oratorical paragon."

His autobiography is full of anedotes and stories from his preaching experiences in many different places. It's a book you won't want to put down until you're finished!

Buy online at our website: **www.KingsleyPress.com**
Also available as an eBook for Kindle, Nook and iBooks.

Made in the USA
San Bernardino, CA
29 July 2014